Copyright © 2025
Yatir Nitzany
All rights reserved.
ISBN-13: 978-1951244699
Printed in the United States of America

Also by Yatir Nitzany

Conversational Spanish Quick and Easy

Conversational French Quick and Easy

Conversational Italian Quick and Easy

Conversational Portuguese Quick and Easy

Conversational German Quick and Easy

Conversational Dutch Quick and Easy

Conversational Norwegian Quick and Easy

Conversational Danish Quick and Easy

Conversational Russian Quick and Easy

Conversational Ukrainian Quick and Easy

Conversational Bulgarian Quick and Easy

Conversational Polish Quick and Easy

Conversational Heew Quick and Easy

Conversational Yiddish Quick and Easy

Conversational Armenian Quick and Easy

Conversational Romanian Quick and Easy

Conversational Arabic Quick and Easy

CONVERSATIONAL LANGUAGES QUICK AND EASY SERIES

Slavic Series

Russian, Ukrainian, Bulgarian and Polish

YATIR NITZANY

Foreword

About Myself

For many years I struggled to learn Spanish, and I still knew no more than about twenty words. Consequently, I was extremely frustrated. One day I stumbled upon this method as I was playing around with word combinations. Suddenly, I came to the realization that every language has a certain core group of words that are most commonly used and, simply by learning them, one could gain the ability to engage in quick and easy conversational Spanish.

I discovered which words those were, and I narrowed them down to three hundred and fifty that, once memorized, one could connect and create one's own sentences. The variations were and are *infinite*! By using this incredibly simple technique, I could converse at a proficient level and speak Spanish. Within a week, I astonished my Spanish-speaking friends with my newfound ability. The next semester I registered at my university for a Spanish language course, and I applied the same principles I had learned in that class (grammar, additional vocabulary, future and past tense, etc.) to those three hundred and fifty words I already had memorized, and immediately I felt as if I had grown wings and learned how to fly.

At the end of the semester, we took a class trip to San José, Costa Rica. I was like a fish in water, while the rest of my classmates were floundering and still struggling to converse. Throughout the following months, I again applied the same principle to other languages—French, Portuguese, Italian, and Arabic, all of which I now speak proficiently, thanks to this very simple technique.

This method is by far the fastest way to master quick and easy conversational language skills. There is no other technique that compares to my concept. It is effective, it worked for me, and it will work for you. Be consistent with my program, and you too will succeed the way I and many, many others have.

CONTENTS

Introduction to the Program 6

Memorization Made Easy 8

Reading and Pronunciation in the Cyrillic Alphabet ……......9

The Russian Language …………………………….............11

The Program ……………………………………….......…... 13

Building Bridges …………………………….....…..……….. 46

Other Useful Tools in the Russian Language …………......54

The Ukrainian Language …………………………........ 56

The Program ……………………………………….......…... 58

Building Bridges …………………………….....…..……….. 94

Other Useful Tools in the Ukrainian Language ………......102

The Bulgarian Language ……………………………….104

The Program ……………………………………….......…... 106

Building Bridges …………………………….....…..……….. 142

Other Useful Tools in the Bulgarian Language …….…......149

The Polish Language ……………………………….…...151

Reading and Pronunciation in the Polish Language ……..153

The Program ……………………………………….......….... 154

Building Bridges …………………………….....…..………....176

Other Useful Tools in the Polish Language …………….....181

Congratulations Now You Are on Your Own............................184

Note from the Author..186

Introduction to the Program

People often dream about learning a foreign language, but usually they never do it. Some feel that they just won't be able to do it while others believe that they don't have the time. Whatever your reason is, it's time to set that aside. With my new method, you will have enough time, and you will not fail. You will actually learn how to speak the fundamentals of the language—fluently in as little as a few days. Of course, you won't speak perfect Russian, Bulgarian, and Polish at first, but you will certainly gain significant proficiency. For example, if you travel to Russia, Bulgaria, or Poland, you will almost effortlessly be able engage in basic conversational communication with the locals in the present tense and you will no longer be intimidated by culture shock. It's time to relax. Learning a language is a valuable skill that connects people of multiple cultures around the world—and you now have the tools to join them.

How does my method work? I have taken twenty-seven of the most commonly used languages in the world and distilled from them the three hundred and fifty most frequently used words in any language. This process took three years of observation and research, and during that time, I determined which words I felt were most important for this method of basic conversational communication. In that time, I chose these words in such a way that they were structurally interrelated and that, when combined, form sentences. Thus, once you succeed in memorizing these words, you will be able to combine these words and form your own sentences. The words are spread over twenty pages. In fact, there are just nine basic words that will effectively build bridges, enabling you to speak in an understandable manner (please see Building

Bridges at the end of every section). The words will also combine easily in sentences, for example, enabling you to ask simple questions, make basic statements, and obtain a rudimentary understanding of others' communications. I have also created Memorization-Made-Easy Techniques for this program in order to help with the memorization of the vocabulary.

My book is mainly intended for basic present tense vocal communication, meaning anyone can easily use it to "get by" linguistically while visiting a foreign country without learning the entire language. With practice, you will be 100 percent understandable to native speakers, which is your aim. One disclaimer: this is *not* a grammar book, though it does address minute and essential grammar rules (please see footnotes at the bottom of every page). Therefore, understanding complex sentences with obscure words in a foreign language is beyond the scope of this book.

People who have tried this method have been successful, and by the time you finish this book, you will understand and be understood in basic conversational language. This is the best basis to learn not only the Slavic languages but any languages. This is an entirely revolutionary, no-fail concept, and your ability to combine the pieces of the "language puzzle" together will come with *great* ease, especially if you use this program prior to beginning a foreign language class.

This is the best program that was ever designed to teach the reader how to become conversational. Other conversational programs will only teach you phrases. But this is the *only* program that will teach you how to create your *own* sentences for the purpose of becoming conversational.

Memorization Made Easy

There is no doubt the three hundred and fifty words in my program are the required essentials in order to engage in quick and easy basic conversation in any foreign language. However, some people may experience difficulty in the memorization. For this reason, I created Memorization Made Easy. This memorization technique will make this program so simple and fun that it's unbelievable! I have spread the words over the following twenty pages. Each page contains a vocabulary table of ten to fifteen words. Below every vocabulary box, sentences are composed from the words on the page that you have just studied. This aids greatly in memorization. Once you succeed in memorizing the first page, then proceed to the second page. Upon completion of the second page, go back to the first and review. Then proceed to the third page. After memorizing the third, go back to the first and second and repeat. And so on. As you continue, begin to combine words and create your own sentences in your head. Every time you proceed to the following page, you will notice words from the previous pages will be present in those simple sentences as well, because repetition is one of the most crucial aspects in learning any foreign language. Upon completion of your twenty pages, *congratulations,* you have absorbed the required words and gained a basic, quick-and-easy proficiency and you should now be able to create your own sentences and say anything you wish in these Slavic languages. This is a crash course in conversational Russian, Ukrainian, Bulgarian and Polish, and it works!

Reading and Pronunciation in the Cyrillic Alphabet

А а pronounced as Ah as in Far

Б б pronounced as Bih as in Bing

В в pronounced as Veh as in Velvet

Г г pronounced as Geh as in Get

Д д pronounced as Deh as in Developer

Е е pronounced as Yeh as in Yell

Ё ё pronounced as Yo as in Yoyo

Ж ж pronounced as Zhe as in Treasure

З з pronounced as Zee as in Zealot

И и pronounced as Ee as in Knee

Й й pronounced as Ee as in soy

К к pronounced as Kah as in copy

Л л pronounced as ehl as in elevator

М м pronounced as Ehm as in blemish

Н н pronounced as Ehn as in pen

О о pronounced as Oh as in snow

П п pronounced as Peh as in pet

Р р pronounced as Ehr as in error

С с pronounced as Ehs as in less

Т т pronounced as Teh as in test

У у pronounced as Oo as in boo

Ф ф pronounced as Ehf as in Left

Х х pronounced as Khah as in Yacht

Ц ц pronounced as Tse

Ч ч pronounced as Che as in Chen

Ш ш pronounced as Shah as in Shop

Щ щ pronounced as Shchah as in Should

Ъ ъ Tvyordeey znahk (hard sign) Letter before is hard

Ы ы Ih Guttural "ee" in the back of the throat

Ь ь Myagkeey znahk (soft sign) Consonant before is soft

Э э pronounced as Eh Net

Ю ю pronounced as Yoo United

Я я pronounced as Yah Yak

Conversational Russian Quick and Easy
The Most Innovative Technique to Learn the Russian Language

YATIR NITZANY

The Russian Language

As many Russian words have Bulgarian roots, Russian is the most common language in Europe and Russia. Perhaps a reason for its popularity is that it also derives vocabulary and connotations from the French, English, German, Latin, and Greek languages. It is also one of the official languages of United Nations. After the Soviet Union fell apart, Russian was only the official language of present-day Russia, and other countries that were part of the Union were encouraged to speak their native tongues. Prior to that, all countries that were part of the Soviet Union were required to speak only Russian, though it still remains the official language of Ukraine, Kazakhstan, Kyrgyzstan, and Belarus. However, Russian is not limited to Europe, as it is the tenth most-spoken language in the United States.

Spoken in: Russia, former Soviet republics

RUSSIAN PRONUNCIATION

In this program, whenever encountering a *t'* at the end of verbs, pronounce it as a soft "ts." For example, "to buy" / *kupit'* is pronounced as "kupits" (with a soft sounding "ts").

Whenever encountering *y'y* or *u'u*, pronounce them as "uo" as in "buoy."

Kh—For the Russian language as well as Middle Eastern languages, including Arabic, Hebrew, Farsi, Pashto, Urdu, Hindi, etc., to properly pronounce the *kh* or *ch* is essential, for example, *nacht* ("night" in German) or *Chanukah* (a Jewish holiday) or *Khaled* (a Muslim name). The best way to describe *kh* or *ch* is to say "ka" or "ha" while at the same time putting your tongue at the back of your throat and blowing air. It's pronounced similarly to the sound that you make while clearing your throat of phlegm. *Please remember this whenever you come across any word containing a *kh* in this program.

Again, this is *not* a pronunciation book. The sole purpose of this book is to provide you with the necessary skills in order to engage in fluent conversational communications. With regards to grammar and pronunciation, you are *on your own!*

The Program

Let's Begin! "Vocabulary" (Memorize the Vocabulary).

I / I am - Ya Я
With you – S toboy С тобой
With us - S nami С нами
For you - Dlya tebya Для тебя
For you - (**Plural**) dla vas для вас
You - (**informal**)Ty Ты
You - (**formal**)vy вы
You - (**plural**)vy вы
Are you / you are - (**informal**)Ty Ты
Are you / you are - (**formal**)vy вы
Are you / you are - (**plural**)vy вы
From - (from a place) Iz Из
From - (from person) ot от
Today - Sehodnya Сегодня
House / home - Dom Дом
Russia - Rossiya Россия
Moscow - Moskva Москва

Sentences composed from the vocabulary you just learned.

Are you at the house?
Ty doma?
Ты дома?

I am always with her
Ya v'segda s ney
Я всегда с ней

I am from Russia
Ya iz Rossii
Я из России

Are you from Moscow?
Ty iz Moskvi?
Ты из Москвы?

Disclaimer: This program doesn't address the nominative, accusative, genitive, dative, instrumental, and prepositional cases since, as it was previously stated, this isn't a grammar book.

With him - S nim С ним
With her - S ney с ней
Without him - Bez nego Без него
Without them - Bez nih Без них
Always - V'segda Всегда
The - (no equivalent)
This, this is - (**Masc**)Etot Этот
This, this is - (**Fem**)Eta Эта,
This, this is - (**Neuter**)Eto Это
This, this is - (**Plural**)Eti Эти
These – Eti Эти
Better - Luchshe Лучше
He, he is - On Он
She, she is – Ona Она
Sometimes – Inogda Иногда
Alone - Odin один
Was - Byl Был
No - Net Нет
Yes - Da Да

Are you alone today?
Ty odin segodnya?
Ты один сегодня?

This is for you
Eto dlya tebya
Это для тебя

Sometimes I go with him
Inogda ya idy s nim
Иногда я иду с ним

I am with you
Ya s toboy/ ya s vami (plural)
Я с тобой/ я с вами

*In Russian, the article "the" doesn't exist nor do the verbs "is" and "are." The article "a" doesn't exist in Russian either.

I was - Ya byl Я был
To be - Byt' Быть
Good/ Okay - Khorosho Хорошо
Here - Zdes' Здесь
Here - Vot вот
Very - Ochen' Очень
And - i (pronounced as ee) и
Between - Mezhdu Между
If - Yesli Если
Now - Sey'chas Сейчас
Same - Tozhe samoye Тоже самое
Tomorrow - Zavtra Завтра

I was here with them
Ya byl zdes' s nimi
Я был здесь с ними

I was home at 5pm
YA byl doma v 5 vechera
Я был дома в 5 вечера

Between now and tomorrow.
Mezhdu seychas i zavtra.
Между сейчас и завтра.

*In regards to the adjectives "this," "that," "its," and "these," if there is a word between these adjectives and the noun, then use eto это. However, if these adjectives are followed by a noun, then their conjugation is according to gender and/or singular and plural: etot этот(m.), eta эта(f.) eto это(n.), eti эти(p.).
"this/that is a girl" / eto devushka это девушка, "this/that girl" / eta devushka эта девушка, "these are girls" / eto devushki этодевушки "these girls" eti devushki эти девушки, "this/that is a boy" / eto mal'chik это мальчик, "this/that boy" etot mal'chik этотмальчик, "these are boys" / eto mal'chiki это мальчики "these boys" eti mal'chiki эти мальчики.

Day - Den' День
It's - (**M**)Etot Этот
It's - (**F**)Eta Эта
It's - (**N**)Eto Это
It's - (**P**)Eti Эти
Later / After - Pozzhe Позже
Later / After - Posle после
Later / After - Pozdno поздно
Yes - Da Да
Then - Zat'em Затем
Good - (person) (**M**)Khoroshiy Хороший
Good - (person) (**F**)khoroshaya хорошая
Happy - Schastlivyy Счастливый

You and I
Ty i ya
Ты и я

It's better to be home later.
Luchshe byt' doma pozzhe.
Лучше быть дома позже.

If this is good, then I am happy.
Yesli eto khorosho, to ya schastliv.
Если это хорошо, то я счастлив.

Yes, you are very good
Da, ty ochen' kharoshiy/kharoshaya
Да, ты очень хороший/хорошая

The same day
Tot zhe den'
Тот же день

*In Russian, whenever "what" is preceded by a noun, you say kakoy какой. <u>kakoy</u> какой(m.) / <u>kakaya</u> какая(f.) / <u>kakoe</u> какое(n.)/ <u>kakie</u> какие(p.)

Maybe - Mozhet byt' Может быть
Even if - Dazhe yesli Даже если
Afterwards - Posle После
Afterwards - Potom потом
Worse - Khuzhe Хуже
Where - Gde Где
Everything - (**person**) vse все,
Everything - (**object**) vsyo всё
Somewhere - Gde-to Где-то
What - Chto? Что?
Almost - Pochti Почти
There - Tam Там

Even if I go now
Dazhe yesli ya idu seychas
Даже если я иду сейчас

Where is everything?
Gdé vs'o?
Где всё?

Maybe somewhere
Mozhet byt' gde-to
Может быть где-то

Where are you?
Gde ty?
Где ты?

What is this?
Chto eto?
Что это?

This is for us.
Eto dlya nas.
Это для нас.

Where is the airport
Gde aeroport
Где аэропорт

Good morning - Dobroye utro Доброе утро
How are you? - Kak dela? Как дела?
Where are you from? - Otkuda ty Откуда ты?
Hello / hi - Zdravstvuyte Здравствуйте
Hello / hi - Privet привет
What is your name? - Kak tvoyo imya? Как твое имя?
How old are you? - Skol'ko tebé lét Сколько тебе лет?
House / home - Dom Дом
In / at – V В / na на

Good morning, how are you today?
Dobroye utro, kak samochuvstviye?
Доброе утро, как самочувствие?

Hello, what is your name?
Privet, kak tebya zovut?
Привет, как тебя зовут?

How old are you?
Skol'ko tebe let?
Сколько тебе лет?

Where are you from?
Otkuda ty?
Откуда ты?

Is this place near?
Eto mesto ryadom?
Это место рядом?

I want to sleep
Ya khochu spat'
Я хочу спать

Where is the book?
Gde kniga?
Где книга?

*In Russian, na на mean "at," "in," "at the." However, v в could have a similar meaning, but it mostly refers to "inside": "at (inside) the mall," "in (inside) the car."

Car - Avtomobil' Автомобиль
Car - Mashina машина
Already - Uzhe Уже
Me - Mne Мне
Son – Syn Сын
Daughter - Doch' Дочь
Daughter - Dochka дочка
Your - Vash Ваш
Your - Tvoy твой
But / however - No Но
Hard - (hard object) Zhostkiy Жосткий
Hard - (difficult) Trudnyy трудный
Still - Yeshcho Ещё
Before – Pered Перед
Before – do togo до того
Yesterday - Vchera Вчера
For - Za За
For - (a person) Dlya Для

She is not in the car, so maybe she is still at the house?
Yeyo net v mashine, tak chto, mozhet byt', ona vse yeshche doma?
Её нет в машине, так что, может быть, она все еще дома?

I am already in the car with your son and daughter
Ya uzhe v avtomobilye s vashim synom i dochkoy
Я уже в автомобиле с вашим сыном и дочкой

This is very hard, but it's not impossible
Eto ochen' trudno, no eto ne nevozmozhno
Это очень трудно, но это не невозможно

He was here yesterday.
On byl zdes' vchera.
Он был здесь вчера.

*In Russian, "what is your name?" is kak tvoyo imya? как твоё имя? Informally, this is kak tibya zovut? как тебя зовут? while formally it is kak vas zavut? как вас зовут?

Thank you - Spasibo Спасибо
That, that is - (**M**)Etot Этот
That, that is - (**F**)Eta Эта
That, that is - (**N**)Eto Это
That, that is - (**P**)Eti Эти
Time - Vremya Время
Not - Ne Не
I am not - Ya ne Я не
Away - Daleko Далеко
Late - Pozdno Позно
Similar - Analogichnyy Аналогичный
Similar - Pokhozhiy Похожий
Our - Nash Наш
Other / Another - (**M**)Drugoy Другой
Other / Another - (**F**)drugaya другая
Side - Storona Сторона
Until - Do До
Without us - Bez nas Без нас

Thank you, Anton.
Spasibo, Anton.
Спасибо, Антон.

I am not here, I am far away
YA ne zdes', ya daleko
Я не здесь, я далеко

That house is similar to ours.
Etot dom pokhozh na nash.
Этот дом похож на наш.

I am from the other side
Ya s drugoy storony
Я с другой стороны

I was here last night
Ya byl zdes vchera vecherom
Я был здесь вчера вечером

I say / I am saying - Ya govoryu Я говорю
What time is it? - Skol'ko vremeni? Сколько времени?
What time is it? - Kotoriy chas? Который час?
I want - Ya khochu Я хочу
Without you - Bez tebya Без тебя
Everywhere - Vezde Везде
I go / I am going - Ya idu Я иду
With - S С
My - (**M**) Moy Мой
My - (**F**) moya моя
Light – Svet Свет
I need - Mne nujno Мне нужно
I see / I am seeing - Ya vizhu Я вижу
Right now - Seychas Сейчас
To - Dlya Для

I am saying no / I say no
Ya govoryu net
Я говорю нет

You need to be at home.
Tebe nuzhno byt' doma.
Тебе нужно быть дома.

I see light outside
Ya vizhu svet snaruzhi
Я вижу свет снаружи

What time is it right now?
Skol'ko vremja seychas?
Сколько время сейчас?

I see this everywhere
Ya vizhu eto vezde
Я вижу это везде

*This isn't a phrase book! The purpose of this book is solely to provide you with the tools to create your own sentences!

Night - Noch' Ночь
Evening - Vecher вечер
Cousin - (**M**)Dvoyurodnyy brat Двоюродный брат
Cousin - (**F**)dvoyurodnaya sistra двоюродная сестра
To see - Videt' Видеть
Outside - Snaruzhi Снаружи
I must - Ya doljen Я должен
During - Vo vremya Во время
Happy - (**M**) Schastliv Счастлив,
Happy - (**F**) Schastliva Счастлива

I am happy without any of my cousins here
YA schastliv bez moikh dvoyurodnykh brat'yev zdes'
Я счастлив без моих двоюродных братьев здесь

I want to see this in the day
Ya khochu uvidet' eto dnyom
Я хочу увидеть это днём

*In Russian, pronouns have different conjugations when relating to gender:

- "her": yeyo её, his: yego его, its: yego его / he: on он, she: ona она, it: ono оно, they: oni они

- "my": moy мой (male), moya моя (female), moyo моё (neutral), moi мои (plural)

- "their": ikh их (same for male, female, formal, informal, and neutral)

- "your": tvoy твой (male), tvoya твоя (female), tvoyo твоё (neutral), tvoi твои (plural) / "your" (singular formal or plural): vash ваш (male), vasha ваша (fem), vashe ваше (neuter), vashi ваши (plural)

- "our": nash наш (male), nashi наша (female), nashi наше (neutral), nashi наши (plural). Note: *Moikh Моих* is the genitive as well as plural accusative form of the pronoun "my." This program doesn't address the nominative, accusative, genitive, dative, instrumental, and prepositional cases since, as it was previously stated, this isn't a grammar book.

Place - Mesto Место
Easy - Legko Легко
To find - Nayti Найти
To look for /to search - Iskat' Искать
Near - Okolo Около
Close - Ryadom Рядом
To wait - Zhdat' Ждать
To sell - Prodat' Продать
To use - Ispol'zovat' Использовать
To know - Znat' Знать
To decide - Reshit' Решить
Between – Mezhdu Между
That - (conjunction) Chto Что

This place is easy to find
Eto mesto lehko nayti
Это место легко найти

I want to wait until tomorrow
Ya khochu podozhdat' do zavtra
Я хочу подождать до завтра

It's easy to sell this table
Etot stol lehko prodat'
Этот стол легко продать

I want to use this
Ya khochu ispol'zovat' eto
Я хочу использовать это

Is it possible to look for this book in the library.
Mozhno li poiskat' etu knigu v biblioteke.
Можно ли поискать эту книгу в библиотеке.

I need to know that everything is ok
Mne nuzhno znat' chto vsyo v poryadke
Мне нужно знать что всё в порядке

*In the last sentence, "that" is used as a conjunction, chto что.

Because - Potomu chto Потому что
Them - Ikh Их
They - Oni Они
Their - Ikh их
Mine - Moyo Моё
To understand - Ponyat' Понять
Problem - Problema Проблема
Problems - Problemy проблемы
I do / I am doing - Ya delayu Я делаю
To do - Sdelat' Сделать
Like this - Tak так
I can - Ya mogu Я могу
To work - Rabotat' Работать

Do it like this!
Delay eto tak!
Делай это так!

That book is mine
Eta kniga moya
Эта книга моя

I need to understand the problem
Mne nuzhno ponyat' problemu
Мне нужно понять проблему

I can work today
Ya mogu rabotat' segodnya
Я могу работать сегодня

I am there with him
Ya tam s nim
Я там с ним

*In Russian, the verb "need" can either be nuzhno нужно or dolzhen должен, occasionally they can be used interchangeably. However, nuzhno нужно is mostly used to signify necessity while dolzhen должен is used to signify being forced to do something.

To buy - Kupit' Купить
Both – Oba Оба
Each / Every – Kazhdyy Каждый
Myself - Sam Сам
Food - Yeda Еда
Water - Voda Вода
Hotel - Otel' Отель
I like - Mne nravitsya Мне нравится
Your - Tvoy Твой
To look - Smotret' Смотреть
To look - Iskat' искать
Outside - Snaruzhi Снаружи
Of – Iz Из

I like this hotel because it's near the beach
Mne nravitsya etot otel', potomu chto on ryadom s plyazhem
Мне нравится этот отель, потому что он рядом с пляжем

I want to look at the view.
YA khochu posmotret' na vid.
Я хочу посмотреть на вид.

I want to buy a bottle of water
Ya khochu kupit' butylku vody
Я хочу купить бутылку воды

I have a view of the city from the hotel
Iz' moyego otelya vid na gorod
Из моего отеля вид на город

I can go outside.
YA mogu vyyti na ulitsu.
Я могу выйти на улицу.

*In Russian, posmotret' посмотреть is "to look" (all around) while smortet' смотреть is more focused.
*In Russian, the definition of nravitsya нравится is "to enjoy."

Parents - Roditeli Родители
Why - Pochemu Почему
To say - Skazat' Сказать
Something - Chto-to Что-то
Ready - Gotovo Готово
Soon - Skoro Скоро
To work - Rabotat' Работать
Who - Kto Кто
There is / There are - Yest' Есть

I like to be at home with my parents
Mne nravitsya byt' doma s moimi roditelyami
Мне нравится быть дома с моими родителями

Why do I need to say something important?
Zachem mne govorit' chto-to vazhnoye?
Зачем мне говорить что-то важное?

I am busy, but I need to be ready soon
Ya zanyat, no ya dolzhen byt' gotov skoro
Я занят, но я должен быть готов скоро

I like to work
Mne nravitsya rabotat'
Мне нравится работать

Who is there?
Kto tam?
Кто там?

I want to know if they are here.
YA khochu znat', zdes' li oni.
Я хочу знать, здесь ли они.

There are seven dolls
Yest' sem' kukol
Есть семь кукол

*In Russian, moimi моими is the instrumental form of the pronoun "my."

How much - Skol'ko stoit Сколько стоит
To take - Vzyat' Взять
With me - So mnoy Со мной
Without me - Bez menya Без меня
Instead - Vmesto Вместо
Only - Tol'ko Только
When - Kogda Когда
I can - Ya mogu Я могу
Can I - Mogu li ya? Могу ли я?
Or - Ili Или
Were - Gde Где
To eat - S'yest' Съесть
To drink - Vypit' Выпить
I love Ya lyublyu Я люблю

How much money do I need to bring with me?
Skol'ko deneg mne nuzhno vzyat' s soboy?
Сколько денег мне нужно взять с собой?

I like to eat bread instead of rice.
YA lyublyu yest' khleb vmesto risa.
Я люблю есть хлеб вместо риса.

Only when you can
Tol'ko kogda ty mozhesh'
Только когда ты можешь

Go there without me.
Idi tuda bez menya.
Иди туда без меня.

*In Russian, whenever pluralizing nouns, the ending changes to an i. For example, "book" / kniga книга, when pluralized, becomes knigi книги. In Russian, in regards to the verb "need" / nuzhno нужно, its ending changes to an i as well whenever indicating plural possession: "I need the books" / mne nuzhny knigi мне нужны книги or "he needs the books" / Emu nuzhny knigi Ему нужны книги, etc.

27

To Drive - Vodit' Водить
Fast - Bystro Быстро
Slow - Medlenno Медленно
Cold - Kholodno Холодно
Hot - Goryacho Горячо
Inside - Vnutri Внутри
To travel - Puteshestvovst' Путешествовать
Since - S С
First - Pervyy Первый
Time – Vremya Время
Times – Vremena Времена
Children - Deti Дети
Children - Rebyata ребята
Yours - Tvoyo Твоё

I need to drive the car very fast or very slowly
Mne nuzhno vodit' mashinu ochen' bystro ili ochen' medlenno
Мне нужно водить машину очень быстро или очень медленно

It is cold in the library
Kholodno v biblioteke
Холодно в библиотеке

I like to eat a hot meal for my lunch.
YA lyublyu yest' goryachuyu yedu na obed.
Я люблю есть горячую еду на обед.

I want to travel the world.
YA khochu puteshestvovat' po miru.
Я хочу путешествовать по миру.

Since the first time
Poskol'ku v pyervyy raz
Поскольку в первый раз

The children are yours
Deti tvoi
Дети твои

To answer - Otvetit' Ответить
To fly - Letat' Летать
To learn - Uchit'sya Учиться
To swim - Plavat' Плавать
To practice - Praktika Практика
To play - Igrat' Играть
To leave - Vyyti Выйти
Many/much/a lot - Mnogiye Многие
I go to - Ya idu v Я иду в
To leave (something) - Ostavlyat Оставлять
Against - Protiv Против

I am against him
Ya protiv nego
Я против него

I need to answer many questions
Mne nuzhno otvetit' na mnogiye voprosy
Мне нужно ответить на многие вопросы

I want to fly today
Ya khochu letet' segodnya
Я хочу лететь сегодня

I need to learn to swim
Mne nuzhno nauchit'sya plavat'
Мне нужно научиться плавать

I want to learn how to play better tennis.
YA khochu nauchit'sya igrat' luchshe v tennis.
Я хочу научиться играть лучше в теннис.

Everything is about the money.
Vse delo v den'gakh.
Все дело в деньгах.

I want to leave my dog at home.
YA khochu ostavit' svoyu sobaku doma.
Я хочу оставить свою собаку дома.

Nobody - Nikto Никто
Us - Nam Нам
We - My мы
To visit – Vizit Визит
To give - Dat' Дать
Which – Kakoy Какой
To meet – Vstrechat Встречать
Someone - Kto-to Кто-то
Just - Tol'ko Только
To walk - Khodit' Ходить
Family - Sem'ya Семья
Than - Chem Чем
Nothing - Nichego Ничего
Week - Nedelya Неделя

Something is better than nothing
Chto-to luchshe chem nichego
Что-то лучше чем ничего

We go each week to visit my family
My idem kazhduyu nedelyu navestit' moyu sem'yu
Мы идем каждую неделю навестить мою семью

I need to give you something
Mne nuzhno dat' tebe chto-to
Мне нужно дать тебе что-то

Do you want to meet someone?
Vy khotite videt' kago-to?
Вы хотите видеть кого-то?

*In Russian, tebe тебе / vam вам is the indirect object pronoun of the pronoun "you," the person who is actually affected by the action that is being carried out. However, tebe тебе is the informal form and vam вам is the formal form.

Friend – Drug Друг
To borrow - Vzat' Взять
To borrow - Odolzhit' одолжить
To look like - Vyglyadet' kak Выглядеть как
Grandfather - Dedushka Дедушка
To want - Khotet' Хотеть
To stay - Ostat'sya Остаться
To continue - Prodolzhat' Продолжать
Way - Put' (road)Путь
Way - Kuda (method) куда
That's why - Vot pochemu Вот почему
I am not going - Ya ne idu Я не иду

Do you want to look like Arnold
Ty khochesh vyglyadet' kak Arnol'd
Ты хочешь выглядеть как Арнольд

I want to borrow this book for my grandfather
Ya khochu vzyat' etu knigu dlya moyego dedushki
Я хочу взять эту книгу для моего дедушки

I want to drive and to continue on this way to my house
Ya khochu dvigat'sya i prodolzhat' idti po etomu puti do moyego doma
Я хочу двигаться и продолжать идти по этому пути до моего дома

I want to stay in St. Petersburg because I have a friend there.
YA khochu ostat'sya v Sankt-Peterburge, potomu chto u menya tam yest' drug.
Я хочу остаться в Санкт-Петербурге, потому что у меня там есть друг.

*Etomu Этому is the dative case of the demonstrative pronoun "this."

*"I want" / ya khochu я хочу and "you want" ty khochesh' ты хочешь.

I have - U menya yest' У меня есть
I have - Ya imeyu я имею
Don't – Ne Не
To show - Pokazat' Показать
To prepare - Podgotovit' Подготовить
How – Kak Как
Also / too / as well - Takzhe Также
Around – Vokrug Вокруг
Russian – Russkiy Русский

I don't want to see anyone here
Ya ne khochu nikogo videt' zdes'
Я не хочу никого видеть здесь

I need to show you how to prepare breakfast
Mne nuzhno pokazat' vam, kak prigotovit' zavtrak
Мне нужно показать вам, как приготовить завтрак

Why don't you have the book?
Pochemu u tebya net knigi?
Почему у тебя нет книги?

I don't need the car today
Mne ne nuzhna mashina segodnya
Мне не нужна машина сегодня

I am here also on Wednesdays
Ya zdes' takzhe po sredam
Я здесь также по средам

You do this every day?
Ty delayesh eto kazhdyy den'?
Ты делаешь это каждый день?

You need to walk around the school.
Vam nuzhno proytis' po shkole.
Вам нужно пройтись по школе.

*In Russian, moyego моего is the masculine and plural accusative form as well as the genitive masculine and neutral form of the pronoun "my."

Hour - Chas Час
Dark - Temno Темно
Darkness - temnota темнота
About - O О
Grandmother - Babushka Бабушка
Five - Pyat' Пять
Minute - Minuta Минута
Minutes - Minuty минуты
More - Bol'she Больше
To think - Dumat' Думать
To come - Priyekhat' Приехать
To hear - Uslyshat' Услышать
Last – Posledniy Последний
To talk / to speak - Govorit' Говорить

This is the last hour of darkness
Eto posledniy chas t'my
Это последний час тьмы

I want to come with you.
YA khochu poyti s toboy.
Я хочу пойти с тобой.

I can hear my grandmother speaking Russian.
YA slyshu, kak moya babushka govorit po-russki.
Я слышу, как моя бабушка говорит по-русски.

I need to think about this more.
Mne nuzhno podumat' ob etom bol'she.
Мне нужно подумать об этом больше.

From here to there, it's only five minutes
Otsyuda do tuda pyat' minut
Отсюда до туда пять минут

*In Russian, "from here" is otsyuda отсюда.

*Etom Этом is the prepositional case of the demonstrative pronoun "this."

To leave - Uyti Уйти
To bring - Prinesti Принести
To try - Popytat'sya Попытаться
To rent - Arendovat' Арендовать
Without her - Bez neyo Без неё
We are - My Мы
To turn off - Vyklyuchit' Выключить
To ask - Sprosit' Спросить
To stop - Ostanovit' Остановить
Permission - Razresheniye Разрешение

He must go and rent a house at the beach.
On dolzhen poyti i snyat' dom na beregu.
Он должен пойти и снять дом на берегу.

I need to turn off the lights early tonight
Vecherom ya dolzhen vyklyuchit' svet rano
Вечером я должен выключить свет рано

We want to stop here
My khotim ostanovitsya zdes'
Мы хотим остановиться здесь

We are from Moscow.
My iz Moskvy.
Мы из Москвы.

Your doctor is in the same building.
Vash vrach nakhoditsya v tom zhe zdanii.
Ваш врач находится в том же здании.

In order to leave you have to ask permission.
Chtoby uyti, nuzhno sprosit' razresheniya.
Чтобы уйти, нужно спросить разрешения.

Come here quickly.
Idi syuda bystro.
Иди сюда быстро.

*In Russian, the definition of na на is "at the."

To return - Vernut'sya Вернуться
Future - Budushcheye Будущее
Door - Dver' Дверь
Our - Nash Наш
On - Na На
Name - Imya Имя
Last name - Familiya Фамилия
Nice to meet you - Priyatno poznakomit'sya
Приятно познакомиться

Nice to meet you, what is your name and your last name?
Priyatno poznakomit'sya s vami, kak vashe imya i vasha familiya?
Приятно познакомиться с вами, как ваше имя и ваша фамилия?

We can hope for a better future.
My mozhem nadeyat'sya na luchsheye budushcheye.
Мы можем надеяться на лучшее будущее.

It is impossible to live without problems.
Nevozmozhno zhit' bez problem.
Невозможно жить без проблем.

I want to return to the United States.
YA khochu vernut'sya v Soyedinennyye Shtaty.
Я хочу вернуться в Соединенные Штаты.

Why are you sad right now?
Pochemu ti grustnaya seychas?
Почему ты грустная сейчас?

Our house is on the mountain.
Nash dom nakhoditsya na gore.
Наш дом находится на горе.

*In Russian, po по means "on."

*This isn't a phrase book! The purpose of this book is solely to provide you with the tools to create your own sentences!

To happen - Sluchit'sya Случиться
To order - Zakazat' Заказать
Excuse me - Izvinite Извините
Child - Rebyonok Ребёнок
Woman - Zhenshchina Женщина
To begin / To start - Nachat' Начать
To finish - Zakonchit' Закончить
To remember - Zapomnit' Запомнить
Number – Nomer Номер

I need to remember this number
Mne nuzhno pomnit' etot nomer
Мне нужно помнить этот номер

This must happen today
Eto dolzhno proizoyti segodnya
Это должно произойти сегодня

Excuse me, my child is here as well
Izvinite, moy rebyonok tozhe zdes'
Извините, мой ребёнок тоже здесь

I want to order a soup.
YA khochu zakazat' sup.
Я хочу заказать суп.

We want to start the class soon.
My khotim poskoreye nachat' zanyatiya.
Мы хотим поскорее начать занятия.

In order to finish at three o'clock this afternoon, I need to finish soon.
Chtoby zakonchit' v tri chasa dnya, mne nuzhno zakonchit' kak mozhno skoreye.
Чтобы закончить в три часа дня, мне нужно закончить как можно скорее.

I want to learn how to speak Russian perfectly.
YA khochu nauchit'sya govorit' po-russki v sovershenstve.
Я хочу научиться говорить по-русски в совершенстве.

To smoke - Kurit' Курить
To love - Lubit' Любить
To help - Pomoch' Помочь
Sun - Solntse Солнце
Exact - Tochnyy Точный
Again - Opyat' Опять
Again - snova снова
I don't - Ya ne Я не

I don't want to smoke again
Ya ne khochu kurit' opyat'
Я не хочу курить опять

I want to help
Ya khochu pomoch'
Я хочу помочь

I love you
Ya tebya lyublyu
Я тебя люблю

I see you
Ya tebya vizhu
Я тебя вижу

I need you
Ty mne nuzhen
Ты мне нужен

There is sun outside today.
Segodnya na ulitse solntse.
Сегодня на улице солнце.

Is it possible to know the exact day?
Mozhno uznat' tochnyy den'?
Можно узнать точный день?

*In Russian, tebya тебя is the "direct object pronoun" of the pronoun you.

To read - Chitat' Читать
To write - Pisat' Писать
To teach - Uchit' Учить
To close - Zakryt' Закрыть
To turn on - Vklyuchit' Включить
To prefer - Predpochitat' Предпочитать
To put - Polozhit' Положить
Less - Men'she Меньше
Month - Mesyats Месяц
I talk - Ya govoryu Я говорю
To choose - Vybirat' Выбирать
In order to - Chtoby Чтобы

I need this book to learn how to read and write in Russian.
Mne nuzhna eta kniga, chtoby nauchit'sya chitat' i pisat' po-russki.
Мне нужна эта книга, чтобы научиться читать и писать по-русски.

I want to teach English in Russian.
YA khochu prepodavat' angliyskiy na russkom yazyke.
Я хочу преподавать английский на русском языке.

I want turn on the lights and close the door.
YA khochu vklyuchit' svet i zakryt' dver'.
Я хочу включить свет и закрыть дверь.

I want to pay less than you.
YA khochu platit' men'she, chem vy.
Я хочу платить меньше, чем вы.

I prefer to put this here.
YA predpochitayu razmeshchat' eto zdes'.
Я предпочитаю размещать это здесь.

I speak with the boy and the girl in Russian
Ya govoryu s mal'chikom i devochkoy po-russki
Я говорю с мальчиком и девочкой по-русски

To exchange - Pomenyat' Поменять
To call - Pozvonit' Позвонить
Brother - Brat Брат
Dad - Papa Папа
To sit - Sidet' Сидеть
Together - Vmeste Вместе
To change - Pomenyat' Поменять
Of course - Konechno Конечно
Welcome - Dobro pozhalovat' Добро пожаловать
During - Vo vremya Во время
Years - Gody Годы
Up - Naverkh Наверх
Down - Vniz Вниз
Big - Bol'shoy Большой
New - Novyy Новый
Never - Nikogda Никогда

I am never able to exchange this money at the bank.
YA nikogda ne smogu obmenyat' eti den'gi v banke.
Я никогда не смогу обменять эти деньги в банке.

I want to call my brother and my dad today
Segodnya ya khochu pozvonit' moemu bratu i moemy pape
Сегодня я хочу позвонить моему брату и моему папе

Of course I can come to the theater, and I want to sit together with you and with your sister
Konechno, ya mogu priyti v teatr, i ya khochu sidet' vmeste s toboy i s tvoyey sestroy
Конечно, я могу прийти в театр, и хочу сидеть вместе с тобой и с твоей сестрой

If you look under the table, you can see the new rug.
Yesli zaglyanut' pod stol, to mozhno uvidet' novyy kover.
Если заглянуть под стол, то можно увидеть новый ковер.

To allow - Razreshit' Разрешить
To believe - Verit' Верить
Morning – Utro Утро
Except - Krome Кроме
To promise - Obeshchat' Обещать
Good night - Spokoynoy nochi Спокойной ночи
To recognize - Priznat' Признать
People - Lyudi Люди
Far - Daleko Далеко
To move (to a place) - Pereyekhat' Переехать`
Sorry - Izvini Извини
To follow - Sledovat' Следовать
Sky - Nebo Небо
To go - Yekhat' Ехать

I need to allow him to go with us.
YA dolzhen pozvolit' yemu poyti s nami.
Я должен позволить ему пойти с нами.

I can't recognize him.
YA ne mogu uznat' yego.
Я не могу узнать его.

I believe everything except for this
Ya veryu vsemu krome etogo
Я верю всему кроме этого

I am sorry.
Mne zhal'.
Мне жаль.

I can see the sky from the window
Ya vizhu nebo iz okna
Я вижу небо из окна

The dog wants to follow me to the store.
Sobaka khochet poyti za mnoy v magazin.
Собака хочет пойти за мной в магазин.

Man - Muschina Мาшина
To enter - Voyti Войти
To receive - Poluchit' Получить
Tonight - Vecherom Вечером
Through - Cherez Через
Him / his – Yego Его
To move - Dvigat'sya Двигаться
Different - Drugoy Другой
To open - Otkryt' Открыть
To buy - Kupit' Купить

I need to open the door for my sister
Mne nujno otkryt' dver' dlya moyey sestry
Мне нужно открыть дверь для моей сестры

I need to buy something
Mne nuzhno chto-to kupit'
Мне нужно что-то купить

He is a different man now.
On teper' drugoy chelovek.
Он теперь другой человек.

I need to move your cat to another chair
Ya dolzhen posadit' vashu koshku na drugoy stul
Я должен посадить вашу кошку на другой стул

I see the sun in the morning from the kitchen
Ya vizhu solntse po utram na kukhne
Я вижу солнце по утрам на кухне

I go into the house from the front entrance and not through the yard.
YA zakhozhu v dom s paradnogo vkhoda, a ne cherez dvor.
Я захожу в дом с парадного входа, а не через двор.

To pay - Platit' Платить
Without - Bez Без
Sister - Sestra Сестра
To hope - Nadeyat'sya Надеяться
To live - Zhit' Жить
Mom – Mama Мама
Mother - Mat' мать
To wish - Zhelat' Желать
Bad - Plokhoy Плохой
To get - Poluchit' Получить
To forget - Zabyt' Забыть
Everybody / Everyone - Vse Все
Although - Khotya Хотя
To feel - Chuvstvovat' Чувствовать
Great - Bol'shoy Большой
To like - Nravitsya Нравиться
In front - Speredi Спереди

I want to meet your brothers.
YA khochu poznakomit'sya s tvoimi brat'yami.
Я хочу познакомиться с твоими братьями.

I don't want to wish anything bad
Ya ne khochu zhelat' nichego plokhogo
Я не хочу желать ничего плохого

I must forget everybody from my past.
YA dolzhen zabyt' vsekh iz moyego proshlogo.
Я должен забыть всех из моего прошлого.

To feel well I must take vitamins.
Chtoby chuvstvovat' sebya khorosho, ya dolzhen prinimat' vitaminy.
Чтобы чувствовать себя хорошо, я должен принимать витамины.

*In Russian, nravitsya нравится means "to enjoy," while lyublyu люблю means "to love."

Person - Chelovek Человек
Behind - Za За
Well – Khorosho Хорошо
Restaurant - Restoran Ресторан
Bathroom - Vannaya komnata Ванная комната
Bathroom - Tualet туалет
Goodbye Do svidaniya До свидания
Next - Sleduyushchiy Следующий

Goodbye my friend.
Proshchay moy drug.
Прощай мой друг.

Which is the best restaurant in the area?
Kakoy luchshiy restoran v etom rayone?
Какой лучший ресторан в этом районе?

I can feel the heat.
YA chuvstvuyu zhar.
Я чувствую жар.

I need to repair a part of the cabinet in the bathroom.
Mne nuzhno otremontirovat' chast' shkafa v vannoy.
Мне нужно отремонтировать часть шкафа в ванной.

I want a car before the next year
Ya khochu mashinu na sleduyushchiy god
Я хочу машину на следующий год

I like the house, however it is very small
 Mne nravitsa dom, no on ochen' malen'kiy
Мне нравится дом, но он очень маленький

I am close to the person behind you
Ya blizhe k cheloveku za toboy
Я ближе к человеку за тобой

*In Russian, sleduyushchiy следующий means "next to," for example, "I am next to him". While sleduyushcheye следующееmeans "the following," for example "the next exit."

Please - Pozhaluysta Пожалуйста
To remove - Udalyat' Удалять
Beautiful - Krasivyy Красивый
To lift - Podnyat' Поднять
Include - Vklucheno, Включено
Including - Vkluchaya включая
Belong - Otsyuda Отсюда
To hold - Derzhat' Держать
To check - Proveryat' Проверять
Small - Malen'kaya Маленькая
Small - Malen'kiy маленький

She wants to remove this door
Ona khochet snyat' etu dver'
Она хочет снять эту дверь

We need to check the size of the house
Mne nuzhno proverit' razmery doma
Мне нужно проверить размеры дома

I want to lift this.
YA khochu podnyat' eto.
Я хочу поднять это.

Can you please put the wood in the fire?
Ne mogli by vy podlozhit' drova v ogon'?
Не могли бы вы подложить дрова в огонь?

This doesn't belong here, I need to check again
Eto ne otsyuda, mne nuzhno proverit' opyat'
Это не отсюда, мне нужно проверить опять

*In Russian the verb "need" has two definitions nado надо and nuzhno нужно. Both signify doing something out of necessity such as "need to," "have to," "should." Both could be used interchangeably however nado надо has more of a colloquial use. On the other hand, dolzhen должен means "must", something you are forced to do. You will notice in some instances, throughout the program, these three Russian verbs being used interchangeably.

Real - Nastoyashchiy Настоящий
Week - Nedelya Неделя
Size - Razmer Размер
Even though - Dazhe yesli Даже если
Doesn't - Net Нет
So - Tak Так
So - Normal'no нормально
Price – Tsena Цена

Is that a real diamond?
Eto nastoyashchiy brilliant?
Это настоящий бриллиант?

This week the weather was very beautiful
Na etoy nedele pogoda byla ochen' khoroshaya
На этой неделе погода была очень хорошая

The sun is high in the sky.
Solntse vysoko v nebe.
Солнце высоко в небе.

I can pay this although the price is expensive
Ya mogu zaplatit' za eto, khotya tsena dorogaya
Я могу заплатить за это, хотя цена дорогая

Can you please hold my hand?
Ne mogli by vy derzhat' menya za ruku?
Не могли бы вы держать меня за руку?

Is everything included in this price?
V etu tsenu vsyo vklucheno?
В эту цену всё включено?

*In Russian, both tak так and normal'no нормально are used to indicate "so". However tak так definition of "so" is used to express cases such as "so much", or "so big." While normal'no нормально definition of "so" is used to indicate "then."

Building Bridges

In Building Bridges, we take the six conjugated verbs that have been selected after studies I have conducted for several months in order to determine which verbs are most commonly conjugated, and which are then automatically followed by an infinitive verb. For example, once you know how to say, "I need," "I want," "I can," and "I like," you will be able to connect words and say almost anything you want more correctly and understandably.

I want - Ya khochu Я хочу
I need - Mne nuzhno / mne nado Мне нужно / мне надо
I can - Ya mogu Я могу
I like - Mne nravitsya Мне нравится
I go - Ya idu Я иду
I have to/ I must - Ya dolzhen Я должен
To have - U menya yest' У меня есть

I want to go to my apartment
Ya khochu poyti v moyu kvartiru
Я хочу пойти в мою квартиру

I can go with you to the bus station
Ya mogu poyti s toboy na avtobusnuyu stantsiyu
Я могу пойти с тобой на автобусную станцию

I need to walk outside the museum.
Mne nuzhno vyyti za predely muzeya.
Мне нужно выйти за пределы музея.

I like to eat oranges.
YA lyublyu yest' apel'siny.
Я люблю есть апельсины.

I want to teach a class
Ya khochu uchit' klass
Я хочу учить класс

I have to speak to my teacher
Ya dolzhen pogovorit' s moim uchitelem
Я должен поговорить с моим учителем

Please master *every* single page up until here prior to attempting the following two pages!

You want - Ty khochesh' Ты хочешь

Do you want? - Khochesh' li ty? хочешь ли ты?

He wants - On khochet Он хочет

Does he want? - Khochet li on? хочет ли он?

She wants - Ona khochet Она хочет

Does she want? - Khochet li ona? хочет ли она?

We want - My khotim Мы хотим

Do we want? - Khotim li my? хотим ли мы?

They want - Oni khotyat Они хотят

Do they want? - Khotyat li oni? хотят ли они?

You (plural/ formal sing) want - Vy khotite Вы хотите

You need - Tebe nuzhno Тебе нужно

Do you need? - Nuzhno li tebe? Нужно ли тебе?

He needs - Yemu nuzhno Ему нужно

Does he need? - Nuzhno li yemu? Нужно ли ему?

She needs - Yey nuzhno Ей нужно

Does she need? - Nuzhno li yey? Нужно ли ей?

We need - Nam nuzhno Нам нужно

Do we need? - Nuzhno li nam? Нужно ли нам?

They need - Im nuzhno Им нужно

Do they need? Nuzhno li im? Нужно ли им?

You (plural/ formal sing) need - Vam nuzhno Вам нужно

You can - Ty mozhesh Ты можешь

Can you? - Mozhesh li ty? Можешь ли ты?

He can - On mozhet Он может

Can he? - Mozhet li on? Может ли он?

She can - Ona mozhet Она может

Can she? - Mozhet li ona? Может ли она?

We can - My mozhem Мы можем

Can we? - Mozhem li my? Можем ли мы?

They can - Oni mogut Они могут

Can they? - Mogut li oni? Могут ли они?

You (plural/ formal sing) can - Vy mozhete Вы можете

You like - Tebe nravitsya Тебе нравится

do you like? - Nravitsya li tebe? Нравится ли тебе?

He likes - Yemu nravitsya Ему нравится

does he like? - Nravitsya li yemu? Нравится ли ему?

She like - Yey nravitsya Ей нравится

does she like? - Nravitsya li yey? Нравится ли ей?

We like - Nam nravitsya Нам нравится

do we like? - Nravitsya li nam? Нравится ли нам?

They like - Im nravitsya Им нравится

do they like? - Nravitsya li im? Нравится ли им?

You (plural/ formal sing) like - Vam nravitsya Вам нравится

You go - Ty idyosh' Ты идёшь

Do you go? - Idyosh' li ty? Идёшь ли ты?

He goes - On idyot Он идёт

Does he go? - Idyot li on? Идёт ли он?

She goes - Ona idyot Она идёт

Does she go? - Idyot li ona? Идёт ли она?

We go - My idyom Мы идём

Do we go? - Idyom li my? Идём ли мы?

They go - Oni idut Они идут

Do they go? - Idut li oni? Идут ли они?

You (plural/ formal sing) go - Vy idyote Вы идёте

You must - Ty dolzhen Ты должен

Do you have to - Dolzhen li ty? Должен ли ты?

He must - On dolzhen Он должен

Does he have to -Dolzhen li on? Должен ли он?

She must - Ona dolzhna Она должна

Does she have to - Dolzhna li ona? Должна ли она?

We have - My dolzhni Мы должны

Do we have to - Dolzhni li my? Должны ли мы?

They must - Oni dolzhni Они должны

Do they have to - Dolzhni li oni? Должны ли они?

You (plural/ formal sing) must - Vy dolzhni Вы должны

You have - Ty imeyesh Ты имеешь

You have - U tebya yest' у тебя есть

He has - On i'meyet Он имеет

He has - U nego yest' у него есть

She has - Ona i'meyet Она имеет

She has - U neyo yest' у неё есть

We have - My imeyem Мы имеем

We have - U nas yest' у нас есть

They have - Oni imeyut Они имеют

They have - U nikh yest' у них есть

You (plural) have - Vy imeyete Вы имеете

You (plural) have - U vas yest' у вас есть

Do you want to go?
Khotite li vy poyti?
Хотите ли вы пойти?

Does he want to fly?
Khochet li on letet'?
Хочет ли он лететь?

We want to swim
My khotim plavat'
Мы хотим плавать

Do they want to run?
Khotyat li oni begat'?
Хотят ли они бегать?

Do you need to clean?
Dolzhna li ty ubrat'?
Должна ли ты убрать?

She needs to sing a song
Ona doljna pet' pesnyu
Она должна петь песню

We need to travel
My dolzhny puteshestvovat'
Мы должны путешествовать

They don't need to fight
Oni ne dolzhny drat'sya
Они не должні драться

You (plural) need to save your money.
Vam nuzhno ekonomit' den'gi.
Вам нужно экономить деньги.

Can you hear me?
Slyshish li ty menya?
Слышишь ли ты меня?

He can dance very well
On mozhet tantsevat' ochen' khorosho
Он может танцевать очень хорошо

We can go out tonight
Me mozhem poyti segodnya vecherom
Мы можем пойти сегодня вечером

The fireman can break the door during an emergency.
Pozharnyy mozhet slomat' dver' vo vremya chrezvychaynoy situatsii.
Пожарный может сломать дверь во время чрезвычайной ситуации.

Do you like to eat here?
Nravitsya li vam zdes' est'?
Нравится ли вас здесь есть?

He likes to spend time here
On lyubit provodit' vremya zdes'
Он любит проводить время здесь

We like to fix the house
My khoteli ispravit' dom
Мы хотели исправть дом

They like to cook
Oni lyubyat gotovit'
Они любят готовить

You (plural) like to play soccer.
Vy lyubite igrat' v futbol.
Вы любите играть в футбол.

Do you go to the movies on weekends?
Khodite li vy v kino po vykhodnym?
Ходите ли вы в кино по выходным?

He goes fishing
On idyot lovit' rybu
Он идёт ловить рыбу

We are going to relax
My sobirayemsya rasslabit'sya
Мы собираемся расслабиться

They go out to eat at a restaurant every day.
Oni khodyat poyest' v restoran kazhdyy den'.
Они ходят поесть в ресторан каждый день.

Do you have money?
Yest' li u tebya den'gi?
Есть ли у тебя деньги?

She must look outside
Ona dolzhna posmoret' snaruzhi
Она должна посмотреть снаружи

We have to sign here
My dolzhny raspisat'sya zdes'
Мы должны расписаться здесь

They have to send the letter
Oni dolzhny otpravit' pis'mo
Они должны отправить письмо

You (plural) have to stand in line.
Vy dolzhny stoyat' v ocheredi.
Вы должны стоять в очереди.

Other Useful Tools in the Russian Language

Days of the Week
Sunday - Voskresen'ye Воскресенье
Monday - Ponedel'nik Понедельник
Tuesday – Vtornik Вторник
Wednesday – Sreda Среда
Thursday – Chetverg Четверг
Friday – Pyatnitsa Пятница
Saturday – Subbota Суббота

Seasons
Spring - Vesna Весна
Summer – Leto Лето
Autumn – Osen' Осень
Winter – Zima Зима

Colors
Black – Chyornyy Чёрный
White - Belyy Белый
Gray - Seryy Серый
Red - Krasnyy Красный
Blue - Siniy Синий
Yellow – Zhyoltyy Жёлтый
Green – Zelyonyy Зелёный
Orange - Orazhevyy Оранжевый
Purple - Fioletovyy Фиолетовый
Brown – Korichnevyy Коричневый

Cardinal Directions
North - Sever Север
South - Yug Юг
East - Vostok Восток
West - Zapad Запад

Numbers
One - Odin Один
Two - Dva Два
Three - Tri Три
Four - Chetyre Четыре
Five - Pyat' Пять

Six - Shest' Шесть
Seven - Sem' Семь
Eight - Vosem' Восемь
Nine - Devyat' Девять
Ten - Desyat' Десять

Transportation
Train - Poyest Поезд
Tram - Tramvay Трамвай
Airplane - Samalyot Самолёт
Car - Masheena Машина
Subway - Mytro Метро
Tram - Tramcai Трамвай
Bus - Aftoboos Автобус
Bus station - Автобусная остановка Avtobusnaya ostanovka
Trolleybus - Tralleybus Троллейбус
Cab/taxi - Taksee Такси
Bicycle - Velosiped Велосипед
Scooter - Samokat Самокат

Travel
Suitcase - Chee-ma-dan Чемодан
Luggage - Ba-gash Багаж
Reservation - Ree-zeer-va-tsi-ya Резервация
Visa - Vee-za Виза
Passport - Pas-part Паспорт
Customs - Ta-mozh-nya Таможня
Tourist - Too-reest Турист (masculine)
Tourist - Too-reest-ka Туристка (feminine)

Conversational Ukrainian Quick and Easy
The Most Innovative Technique to Learn the Ukrainian Language

YATIR NITZANY

The Ukrainian Language

The East Slavic language of Ukrainian has been the subject of a ban and derision by the Russians and often denied the status of a language in its own right. A quote attributed to Czar Nicholas II goes, "There is no Ukrainian language, just illiterate peasants speaking Little Russian," even though the Ukrainian and Russian lexicons differ by 38% (as opposed to 33% for Spanish and Italian). Outside of Russia, Ukrainian and Russian are accepted as two similar but different languages.

Ukrainian is the official state language of Ukraine and the Crimea, the first of two principal languages for Ukrainians, and one of three official languages for the unrecognized state of Transnistria, of which the other two are Romanian and Russian. It is also a recognized minority language in Bosnia and Herzegovina, Croatia, Czech Republic, Hungary, Moldova, Poland, Romania, Serbia, and Slovakia.

Written Ukrainian uses a variant of the Cyrillic script and there are an estimated forty-five million speakers of the language.

Historical linguists trace the origin of the Ukrainian language to the Old East Slavic, from which it split off about a thousand years ago, of the early medieval state of Kievan Rus'. After the fall of the Kievan Rus' as well as the Kingdom of Galicia–Volhynia, the language developed into a form called the Ruthenian language. The Modern Ukrainian language has been in common use since the late seventeenth century and has been associated with the establishment of the Cossack Hetmanate.

From 1804 until the Russian Revolution, the Ukrainian language was banned from schools in the Russian Empire, of which the biggest part of Ukraine (Central, Eastern, and Southern) was a part at the time. It has always maintained a sufficient base in Western Ukraine, where the language was never banned, in its folklore songs, itinerant musicians, and prominent authors.

The Ukrainian language can be mutually understood, to a degree, by those speaking Belarusian and Russian.

Memorize the vocabulary:

I / I am - Ya Я
With you - Z toboyu З тобою
With us - Z namy З нами
For you - Dlya tebe Для тебе
For you - **(Plural)** dlya vas для вас
Are you / you are - **(informal)** Ty Ти
Are you / you are - **(formal)** vy ви
Are you / you are - **(plural)** vy ye ви є
You - **(informal)** Ty Ви
You - **(formal)** vy ви
You - **(plural)** vy ви
From - *(from a place)* Z З, *(from person)* Vid Від

Sentences composed from the vocabulary you just learned"

I am from Ukraine
Ya z Ukrayiny
Я з України

Are you from Kiev?
Ty z Kyyeva?
Ти з Києва

I am with you
Ya z toboyu/ ya z vamy (plural)
Я з тобою / я з вами

This is for you
Tse dlya tebe
Це для тебе

*In Ukrainian, the soft sign (apostrophe in the transcribed word) after a consonant letter makes that letter softer.

*This *isn't* a phrase book! The purpose of this book is *solely* to provide you with the tools to create *your own* sentences!

With him - Z nym З ним
With her - Z neyu З нею
Without him - Bez n'ogo Без нього
Without them - Bez nyh Без них
Always - Zavzhdy Завжди
This, This is - (**Masc**)Tsey Цей
This, This is - (**Fem**)Tsya Ця,
This, This is - (**Neuter**)Tse Це
This, This is - (**Plural**)Tsi Ці
It is - (**M**)Tsey Цей
It is - (**F**)Tsya Ця
It is - (**N**)Tse Це
It is - (**P**)Tsi Ці
Sometimes - Inodi Іноді
He – Vin Він
She - Vona Вона
Today - S'ogodni Сьогодні
There – Tam Там

Are you at the house?
Vy vdoma?
Ви вдома?

I am always with her
Ya zavzhdy z neyu
Я завжди з нею

Are you alone today?
Ty s'ohodni odna?
Ти сьогодні одна?

Sometimes I go without him.
Inodi ydu bez n'oho.
Іноді йду без нього.

I am there with him
Ya tam z nym
Я там з ним

Was - Buv Був
I was - Ya buv Я був
To be - Buty Бути
Here - Tut Тут
Here - Os' ось
Very - Duzhe Дуже
And - i *(pronounced as ee)* і
Between - Mizh Між
If - Yakshcho Якщо
Now – Zaraz Зараз
Now – Teper тепер
Tomorrow - Zavtra Завтра
Where are you from? – Zvidky ty? Звідки ти?
How old are you? – Skil'ky tobi rokiv? Скільки тобі років?

I was here with them
Ya buv/bula tut z nymy
Я був/була тут з ними

You and I
Ty i ya
Ти і я

I was home at 5pm
YA buv vdoma o 5 vechora
Я був вдома о 5 вечора

Between now and tomorrow.
Mizh teper i zavtra.
Між тепер і завтра.

Where are you from?
Zvidky ty?
Звідки ти?

How old are you?
Skil'ky tobi rokiv?
Скільки тобі років?

The – (no equivalent)
A - (no equivalent)
Later / After – Piznishe Пізніше
Later / After – Pislya після
After - Pislya Після
Afterwards - Piznishe Пізніше
Afterwards - Potim потім
Yes - Tak Так
To - Do До
Happy - (M) Shchaslyvyy Щасливий
Happy - (F) Shchaslyva Щаслива
Better - Krashche Краще
Day - Den' День
Then – Potim Потім
Good morning – Dobrogo ranku Доброго ранку
How are you? – Yak spravy? Як справи?
Good - (M) Dobryy Добрий
Good - (F) Dobra Добра
Same – Te same Те саме
Same – Te zh те ж

It's better to be home later.
Krashche buty vdoma piznishe.
Краще бути вдома пізніше.

If this is good, then I am happy.
Yakshcho tse dobre, to ya shchaslyvyy.
Якщо це добре, то я щасливий.

Yes, you are very good
Tak, ty duzhe dobryy/dobra
Так, ти дуже добрий /добра

The same day
Togo zh dnya
Того ж дня

*In Ukrainian the article "a" and "the" don't exist.

Where - De Де
Okay - Dobre Добре
Everything - (**person**) vsi всі
Everything - (**object**) vse все
Somewhere – Des' Десь
Maybe – Mozhe buty Може бути
What - Shcho? Що?
Almost - Mayzhe Майже
I go - Ya idu Я іду
Worse - Girshe Гірше
Even if – Navit' yakshcho Навіть якщо
No - Nemaye Немає

This is for us.
Tse dlya nas.
Це для нас.

Even if I go now
Navit' yakshcho ya pidu zaraz
Навіть якщо я піду зараз

I am almost there
YA mayzhe tam
Я майже там

Where are you?
De ty?
Де ти?

Where is everything?
De vse?
Де все?

Maybe somewhere
Mozhe des'
Може десь

What is this?
Shcho tse?
Що це?

Already - Vzhe Вже
Son - Syn Син
Daughter - Dochka Дочка
To have - Maty Мати
Doesn't - Ne robyt′ Не робить
Hard – Zhorstkyy Жорсткий(*hard object*)
Hard – Vazhko Важко(*difficult*)
Easy - Lehko Легко
Still – Dosi Досі
Impossible - Nemozhlyvo Неможливо
House - Dim Дім
Home - Dim Дім
In - V, В
In - В, У
At - Bilya Біля
Car – Avtomobil' Автомобіль
Car – Mashyna Машина
Book – Knyga Книга
Isn't – Ne ye Не є

She is not in the car, so maybe she is still at the house?
Yiyi nemaye v mashyni, to mozhe vona shche vdoma?
Її немає в машині, то може вона ще вдома?

I am already in the car with your son and daughter
Ya vzhe v mashyni z vashym synom i dochkoyu
Я вже в машині з вашим сином і дочкою

This is very hard, but it's not impossible
Tse duzhe vazhko, ale tse ne
Це дуже важко, але це не неможливо

*In Ukrainian, to indicate "hard" we use *zhorstkyy жорсткий* or *vazhko важко*. *Zhorstkyy Жорсткий* indicates "hard" as in "a hard object" while *vazhko важко* indicates "hard" as in difficulty.

Thank you - Dyakuyu Дякую
For – Za За
For - (a person) Dlya Для
That, that is - (M) Tsej Цей
That, that is - (F) Tsya Ця
That, that is - (N) Tse Це
That, that is - (P) Tsi Ці
But / however - Ale Але
No - Ni Ні
Not - Ni Ні
Away - Daleko Далеко
Similar - Analogichnyy Аналогічний
Similar - Podibnyy Подібний
Our / ours - Nash Наш
Church - Tserkva Церква

Thank you, Anton.
Dyakuyu, Anton.
Дякую, Антон.

I am not here, I am far away
Mene tut nemaye, ya daleko
Мене тут немає, я далеко

That house is similar to ours.
Toy budynok skhozhyy na nash.
Той будинок схожий на наш.

Where is the Church?
De Tserkva?
Де Церква?

Where is the American embassy?
De amerykans′ke posol′stvo?
Де американське посольство?

*This *isn't* a phrase book! The purpose of this book is *solely* to provide you with the tools to create *your own* sentences!

I say / I am saying - Ya govoryu Я говорю
What time is it? – Kotra godyna? Котра година
I want - Ya khochu Я хочу
Without you - Bez tebe Без тебе
Everywhere – Skriz' Скрізь
I go / I am going - Ya ydu Я йду
I am not going - Ya ne idu Я не іду
With - Z З
My - (M) Miy Мій
My - (F) moya моя
Light - Svitlo Світло
I need - Meni treba Мені треба
I need - Meni potribno Мені потрібно
I see / I am seeing - Ya bachu Я бачу
Right now - Zaraz Зараз

I am saying no / I say no
Ya govoryu ni
Я говорю ні

You need to be at home.
Tobi treba buty vdoma.
Тобі треба бути вдома.

I see light outside house
Ya bachu svitlo zovni/nazovni budynka
Я бачу світло зовні/назовні будинка

What time is it right now?
Kotra zaraz godyna?
Котра зараз година?

I see this everywhere
Ya bachu tse skriz'
Я бачу це скрізь

I see the sun today
Ya bachu sontse syogodni
Я бачу сонце сьогодні

To see - Bachyty Бачити
To understand - Zrozumity Зрозуміти
Outside - Zovni Зовні
Without - Bez Без
Happy – Shchaslyva Щаслива
Other / Another - (M) Drugyy Другий
Other / Another - (F) Insha/druga друга
Side - Storona Сторона
Until - Do До
Yesterday - Vchora Вчора
Without us - Bez nas Без нас
Since - Z З
Day – Den' День
Before – Do До
Late - Pizno Пізно
Person - Lyudyna Людина

I was here last night
Ya buv tut mynuloyi nochi
Я був тут минулої ночі

I am from the other side
Ya z inshoyi storony
Я з іншої сторони

I want to see this in the day
Ya khochu bachyty tsey den'
Я хочу бачити цей день

I understand
Ya rozumiju
Я розумію

I don't understand
Ya ne rozumiju
Я не розумію

*With the knowledge you've gained so far, now try to create your own sentences!

Place - Mistse Місце
Easy - Lehko Легко
To find - Znayty Знайти
To look for - Shukaty Шукати
To search - Shukaty Шукати
To wait - Chekaty Чекати
To sell - Prodaty Продати
To use - Vykorystovuvaty Використовувати
To decide - Vyrishuvaty Вирішувати
Night - Nich Ніч
Evening – Vechir Вечір

This place is easy to find
Tse mistse lehko znayty
Це місце легко знайти

I want to wait until tomorrow
Ya khochu pochekaty do zavtra
Я хочу почекати до завтра

It's easy to sell this table
Tse duzhe lehko prodaty tsey stil
Це дуже легко продати цей стіл

I want to use this
Ya khochu tse vykorystovuvaty
Я хочу це використовувати

Where is the book?
De knyzhka?
Де книжка?

I need to look for you at the mall.
Meni potribno shukaty tebe v torhovomu tsentri.
Мені потрібно шукати тебе в торговому центрі.

I need to be there at night
Meni treba buty tam u vecheri
Мені треба бути там у вечері

Because - Tomu shcho Тому що
Because - Bo Бо
Them - Yim Їм
They - Vony Вони
Their - Yikh Їх
These - Tsi Ці
Mine – Miy Мій
Mine – Moya Моя
Mine – Moye Моє
Mine – Moyi Мої
Myself – Sam Сам
Myself – Sama Сама
To understand - Zrozumity Зрозуміти
Problem - Problema Проблема
I do / I am doing - Ya roblyu Я роблю
Of - Z З
To look - Dyvytys' Дивитись
To look - Shukaty Шукати
To do - Robyty Робити
Near / Close – Blyz'ko Близько

Is this place near?
Tse mistse poblyzu?
Це місце поблизу?

I do what I want.
YA roblyu, shcho khochu.
Я роблю, що хочу.

That book is mine.
Tsya knyha moya.
Ця книга моя.

I need to understand the problem
Meni potribno zrozumity problemu
Мені потрібно зрозуміти проблему

Enough - Dostatn′o Достатньо
To buy - Kupyty Купити
Food - Yizha Їжа
Water - Voda Вода
Each / Every - Kozhnyy Кожний
Everybody / Everyone - Vsi Всі
Everybody / Everyone - Kozhen Кожен
Hotel - Gotel' Готель
Both - Obydva Обидва
Like this - Os' tak Ось так
That's why - Os' chomu Ось чому

I like this hotel because it's near the beach
Meni podobayet′sya tsey gotel′, tomu shcho vin nedaleko vid plyazhu
Мені подобається цей готель, тому що він недалеко від пляжу

I want to look at the view.
YA khochu podyvytysya na krayevyd.
Я хочу подивитися на краєвид.

I want to buy a cup of water
Ya khochu kupyty sklyanku vody
Я хочу купити склянку води

Do it like this!
Zrobit′ tse tak!
Зробіть це так!

I have a view of the city from the hotel
Z gotelyu ya mayu vyd na misto
З готелю я маю вид на місто

*In Ukrainian if you use a separate "why," it will be *chomu чому*. "That's why," transforms into *tomu тому*.

I like - Meni podobayet'sya Мені подобається
Family - Sim'ya Сім'я
Parents - Bat'ky Батьки
Why - Chomu Чому
To say - Skazaty Сказати
Something - Shchos' Щось
To go - Yty Йти
To work -Pratsyuvaty Працювати
Who - Khto Хто
Important – Vazhlyvo Важливо
Hello / hi – Pryvit Привіт
Hello / hi – Dobrogo dnya Доброго дня
What is your name? – Yak tebe zvaty? Як тебе звати?
Your - Vash Ваш
Your - Tviy Твій

Hello, what is your name?
Pryvit, yak tebe zvaty?
Привіт, як тебе звати?

I like to be at home with my parents
Meni podobayet'sya buty doma z moimy bat'kamy
Мені подобається бути дома з моїми батьками

Why do I need to say something important?
Navishcho meni hovoryty shchos' vazhlyve?
Навіщо мені говорити щось важливе?

I like to work
Meni podobayet'sya pratsyuvaty
Мені подобається працювати

Who is there?
Khto tam?
Хто там?

*In Ukrainian, "what is your name?" is *yake tvoye imya? яке твоє ім'я?* Informally, this is *yak tebe zvaty? як тебе звати?*, while formally it is *yak vas zvaty? як вас звати?*

To know - Znaty Знати
There is / There are - Isnuye Існує
There is / There are - Isnuyut' Існують
Ready - Gotovo Готово
Soon - Skoro Скоро
That - (*conjunction*) Shcho Що
Busy – Zanyatyy Занятий

I am busy, but I need to be ready soon
Ya zanyatyy, ale ya povynen buty gotovyy skoro
Я , але я повинен бути готовий скоро

I want to know if they are here.
YA khochu znaty, chy vony tut.
Я хочу знати, чи вони тут.

I can go outside.
YA mozhu vyyty na vulytsyu.
Я можу вийти на вулицю.

There are seven dolls
Ye sim lyal'ok
Є сім ляльок

I need to know that everything is ok
Meni treba znaty shcho vse dobre
Мені треба знати що все добре

*In the last sentence, "that" is used as a conjunction, *shcho що*.

*In Ukrainian, pronouns have different conjugations when relating to gender:
"her": *yiyi її*, his: *yogo його*, its: *yikh їх* / he: v*in він*, she: v*ona вона*, it: v*ono воно*, they: v*ony вони*
"my": *miy мій* (male), *moya моя* (female), *moye моє* (neutral), *moyi мої* (plural)
"their*"*: *yikh їх* (same for male, female, formal, informal, and neutral)

How much - Skil'ky koshtuye Скільки коштує
To bring - Prynesty Принести
With me - Zi mnoyu Зі мною
Only - Til'ky Тільки
When - Koly Коли
I can - Ya mozhu Я можу
Can I? - Chy ya mozhu? Чи я можу?
Were - Buly Були
Without me - Bez mene Без мене
Our - Nash Наш
On – Na На

I can work today
Ya mozhu pratsyuvaty s'ogodni
Я можу працювати сьогодні

Only when you can
Til'ky koly ty mozhesh
Тільки коли ти можеш

They were without me yesterday
Vony buly bez mene vchora
Вони були без мене вчора

How much money do I need to bring with me?
Skil'ky hroshey meni potribno vzyaty z soboyu?
Скільки грошей мені потрібно взяти з собою?

Our house is on the mountain.
Nasha khata na hori.
Наша хата на горі.

*In Ukrainian, pronouns have different conjugations when relating to gender: "your": *tviy твій* (male), *tvoya твоя*(female), *tvoye твоє* (neutral), *yikh їх* (plural) /"your" (singular formal or plural): *vash ваш* (male), *vasha ваша* (fem), *vashe ваше* (neuter), *vashi ваші* (plural) /"our": *nash наш* (male), *nashi наша* (female), *nashi наше* (neutral), *nashi наші*(plural)

Fast - Shvydko Швидко
Slow - Povil'no Повільно
Cold - Kholodno Холодно
Instead - Zamist' Замість
Inside - Vseredyni/v/u Всередині / в / у
To eat - Yisty Їсти
Hot - Haryachyy Гарячий
To Drive – Vodyty Водити
Cousin - (M) Dvoyuridnyy brat Двоюрідний брат
Cousin - (F)dvoyuridna sestra двоюрідна сестра
Or - Abo Або

I like bread instead of rice.
YA lyublyu khlib zamist' rysu.
Я люблю хліб замість рису.

I need to drive the car very fast or very slowly
Meni potribno vodyty mashynu duzhe shvydko abo duzhe povil'no
Мені потрібно водити машину дуже швидко або дуже повільно

It is cold in the library
Kholodno v bibliotetsi
Холодно в бібліотеці

I like to eat a hot meal for my lunch.
YA lyublyu yisty haryachu yizhu na obid.
Я люблю їсти гарячу їжу на обід.

I am happy without any of my cousins here
YA shchaslyvyy, koly tut nemaye moyikh dvoyuridnykh brativ
Я щасливий, коли тут немає моїх двоюрідних братів

Note: *Moikh Моїх* is the genitive as well as plural accusative form of the pronoun "my." This program doesn't address the nominative, accusative, genitive, dative, instrumental, and prepositional cases since, as previously stated, this isn't a grammar book.

To answer - Vidpovisty Відповісти
To fly - Litaty Літати
To travel - Podorozhuvaty Подорожувати
To learn - Navchytysya Навчитися
How – Yak Як
Many/much/a lot - Bagato Багато
I go to - Ya ydu do Я йду до
First - Pershyy Перший
World – Svit Світ
Around - Navkolo Навколо
Yours - Tvoye Твоє
To walk - Khodyty Ходити
Children - Dity Діти
School – Shkola Школа

Since the first time
Z pershogo razu
З першого разу

The children are yours
Tvoyi dity
Твої діти

I need to answer many questions
Meni treba vidpovisty na bagato pytan'
Мені потрібно відповісти на багато питань

I want to fly today
Ya khochu litaty s'ogodni
Я хочу літати сьогодні

You need to walk around the school.
Vam potribno progulyatysya navkolo shkoly.
Вам потрібно прогулятися навколо школи.

*In Ukrainian there are 3 definitions for "time":
Time - Kotra Котра (reference to; hour, "what time is it?")
Time - Chasu Часу (era, moment period, duration of time)
Time – Raz Раз (occasion or frequency)

To swim - Plavaty Плавати
To practice - Praktykuvaty Практикувати
To play - Graty Грати
To leave - Zalyshyty Залишити
To leave - Pity Піти
To talk / to speak – Hovoryty Говорити
How – Yak Як
Better – Krashche Краще
English - Anhliys′ka Англійська

Everything is about the money.
Vsya sprava v hroshakh.
Вся справа в грошах.

I want to leave my dog at home.
YA khochu zalyshyty sobaku vdoma.
Я хочу залишити собаку вдома.

I want to travel the world.
YA khochu podorozhuvaty svitom.
Я хочу подорожувати світом.

I need to learn to swim
Meni potribno navchytysya plavaty
Мені потрібно навчитися плавати

I want to learn how to play better tennis.
YA khochu navchytysya krashche hraty v tenis.
Я хочу навчитися краще грати в теніс.

How do you say that in Ukrainian?
Yak tse skazaty ukrayins′koyu?
Як це сказати українською?

Do you speak English?
Vy hovoryte anhlijs'koju
Ви говорите англійською?

Please speak slowly.
Bud′ laska, govorit′ povil′no.
Будь ласка, говоріть повільно.

Against - Proty Проти
Us - Nam Нам
We - My Ми
To visit - Vidvidaty Відвідати
To repeat - Povtoryty Повторити
Mom / Mother - Mama Мама
To give - Davaty Давати
Just - Til'ky Тільки
Week – Tyzhden' Тиждень
Than - Nizh Ніж
Nothing - Nichogo Нічого

Something is better than nothing
Shchos' krashche nizh nichogo
Щось краще ніж нічого

I am against him
Ya proty n'ogo
Я проти нього

You do this every day?
Ty robysh tse kozhnogo dnya?
Ти робиш це кожного дня?

We go to visit my family every week
My yizdymo kozhen tyzhden' vidviduvaty moyu rodynu
Ми їздимо кожен тиждень відвідувати мою родину

I need to give you something
Meni potribno daty tobi shchos'
Мені потрібно дати тобі щось

Could you repeat?
Povtoreet, bud laska.
Повторіть, будь ласка.

*In Ukrainian, *tobi тобі* / *vam вам* are the indirect object pronouns of the pronoun "you," the person who is actually affected by the action that is being carried out. *Vam Вам* is the formal and *tobi тобі* is the informal variant.

Towards – Nazustrich Назустріч
To meet - Zustrity Зустріти
Someone - Khtos' Хтось
Also / too / as well – Takozh Також
Also / too / as well – Tezh Теж
Wednesday – Sereda Середа
To drink - Pyty Пити
Woman - Zhinka Жінка
To begin / To start - Rozpochaty Розпочати
To finish - Zakinchuvaty Закінчувати
In order to – Shchob Щоб

Do you want to meet someone?
Ty khochesh zustrity kogos'?
Ти хочеш зустріти когось?

We want to start the class soon.
My khochemo nezabarom pochaty zanyattya.
Ми хочемо незабаром почати заняття.

In order to finish at three o'clock this afternoon, I need to finish soon
Shchob zakinchyty s'ohodni o tretiy hodyni dnya, meni potribno zakinchyty shvydshe
Щоб закінчити сьогодні о третій годині дня, мені потрібно закінчити швидше

Have a nice meal
Smačnoho
Смачного!

Have a good journey
Ščaslyvoji podoroži
Щасливої подорожі

I have - U mene ye У мене є
I have - Ya mayu я маю
Don't - Ne treba Не треба
Friend - Druzhe Друже
To borrow - Pozychyty Позичити
Grandfather - Didus' Дідусь
To want - Khotity Хотіти
To stay - Zalyshytysya Залишатися
To continue - Prodovzhyty Продовжити
Way - *(road)* ShlyakhШлях
Way - *(method)* Zasib засіб
To do - Robyty Робити
Nobody - Nikhto Ніхто

I am here also on Wednesdays
Ya tut takozh po seredam
Я тут також по середам

I want to borrow this book for my grandfather
Ya khochu pozychyty tsyu knygu dlya mogo didusya
Я хочу позичити цю книгу для мого дідуся

Why don't you have the book?
Chomu ty ne mayesh knygy?
Чому ти не маєш книгу?

I want to stay in Odessa because I have a friend there.
YA khochu zalyshytysya v Odesi, tomu shcho u mene tam ye druh.
Я хочу залишитися в Одесі, тому що у мене там є друг.

How much is this?
Skiľky ce koštuje?
Скільки це коштує?

*In Ukrainian, to indicate "way" we use *shlyakh* шлях or *zasib* засіб. *Shlyakh* Шлях indicates "road" while *zasib* засібindicates "method."

Anyone - Nikhto Ніхто
To look like - Vyglyadaty yak Виглядати як
To talk / to speak – Hovoryty Говорити
To show - Pokazaty Показати
To prepare - Pidgotuvaty Підготувати
To come - Pryhodyty Проходити
I don't - Ya ne Я не
Do you want? - Ty khochesh Ти хочеш
About - Pro Про
On the - Na На
Ukrainian – Ukrayins′ka Українська

Do you want to look like Arnold?
Ty khochesh vyglyadaty yak Arnol'd?
Ти хочеш виглядати як Арнольд?

I don't want to see anyone here
Ya ne khochu nikogo bachyty tut
Я не хочу нікого бачити тут

I need to show you how to prepare breakfast
Meni treba pokazaty vam, yak prygotuvaty snidanok
Мені треба показати вам, як приготувати сніданок

I don't need the car today
Meni ne potribna s'ogodni mashyna
Мені не потрібна сьогодні машина

I want to come with you.
YA khochu pity z toboyu.
Я хочу піти з тобою.

Do you speak Ukrainian?
Vy rozmovliajete ukrajinśkoju?
Ви розмовляєте українською?

*With the knowledge you've gained so far, now try to create your own sentences!

To remember - Zapam'yataty Запам'ятати
Number - Nomer Номер
Hour - Hodyna Година
Dark / darkness - Temno Темно
Dark / darkness - Pit'ma пітьма
Grandmother - Babusya Бабуся
Five - P'yat' П'ять
Minute - Khvylyna Хвилина
Minutes - Khvylyny хвилини
More - Bil'she Більше
To think - Dumaty Думати
To hear - Slukhaty Слухати
Last – Ostanniy Останній
Last – Mynulyy Минулий

I need to remember this number
Meni potribmo zapam'yataty tsey nomer
Мені потрібно запам'ятати цей номер

This is the last hour of darkness
Tse ostannya hodyna temryavy
Це остання година темряви

I can hear my grandmother speaking Ukrainian.
YA chuyu, yak babusya hovoryt' ukrayins'koyu.
Я чую, як бабуся говорить українською.

I need to think about this more.
Meni potribno bil'she dumaty pro tse.
Мені потрібно більше думати про це.

From here to there, it's only five minutes
Zvidsy tudy vs'oho p'yat' khvylyn
Звідси туди всього п'ять хвилин

*In Ukrainian, the definition of *zvidsy звідси* means "from here."

Again - Znovu Знову
To take - Vzyaty Взяти
To try - Sprobuvaty Спробувати
To rent - Orenduvaty Орендувати
To happen - Statysya Статися
Without her - Bez neyi Без неї
To turn off - Vymknuty Вимкнути
To turn on - Vmykaty Вмикати
To ask - Zapytaty Запитати
To stop - Zupynyty Зупинити
Early - Ranniy Ранній
Beach – Plyazh Пляж
Tonight - S'ohodni vvecheri Сьогодні ввечері
Why - Chomu Чому
Sad – Sumno Сумно

He must go and rent a house at the beach.
Yomu potribno orenduvaty budynok na plyazhi
Йому потрібно орендувати будинок на пляжі

I need to turn off the lights early tonight
S'ohodni vvecheri ya povynen vymknuty svitlo rano
Сьогодні ввечері я повинен вимкнути світло рано

We want to stop here
My khochemo zupynytysya tut
Ми хочемо зупинитися тут

This must happen today
Tse povynno statysya s'ogodni
Це повинно статися сьогодні

Why are you sad right now?
Chomu ty sumna zaraz?
Чому ти сумна зараз?

What do you want?
Shcho ty khochesh?
Що ти хочеш?

Permission – Dozvil Дозвіл
Building - Budivlya Будівля
Doctor - Likar Лікар
Exact - Tochno Точно
In order to – Shchob Щоб
Airport - Aeroport Аеропорт
Sleep - Spaty Спати
Ukraine - Ukrayina Україна
We are - My ye Ми є
To order - Zamovyty Замовити

I want to order a soup.
YA khochu zamovyty sup.
Я хочу замовити суп.

We are from Ukraine.
My z Ukrayiny.
Ми з України.

Your doctor is in the same building.
Vash likar znakhodyt′sya v tiy zhe budivli.
Ваш лікар знаходиться в тій же будівлі.

In order to leave you have to ask permission.
Shchob vyyikhaty, potribno zapytaty dozvolu.
Щоб виїхати, потрібно запитати дозволу.

Is it possible to know the exact day?
Mozhna diznatysya tochnyy den'?
Можна дізнатися точний день?

Where is the airport?
De aeroport?
Де аеропорт?

I want to sleep
Ya khochu spaty
Я хочу спати

To open - Vidkryvaty Відкривати
To pay - Platyty Платити
To buy - Kupuvaty Купувати
To hope - Spodivatysya Сподіватися
To get to know – Poznayomytysya Познайомитися
A bit, a little, a little bit - Trokhy Трохи
Sister - Sestra Сестра
Name - Im'ya Ім'я
Last name - Prizvyshche Прізвище
Door - Dveri Двері
Future - Maybutnye Майбутнє
Nice to meet you - Pryyemno poznayomytys′
Приємно познайомитись

I need to open the door for my sister
Meni potribno vidchynyty dveri dlya moyeyi sestry
Мені потрібно відчинити двері для моєї сестри

I need to buy something
Meni potribno shchos' kupyty
Мені потрібно щось купити

I want to meet your brothers.
YA khochu poznayomytysya z vashymy bratamy.
Я хочу познайомитися з вашими братами.

Nice to meet you, what is your name and your last name?
Pryyemno poznayomytysya z vamy, yak vas zvaty i yake vashe prizvyshche?
Приємно познайомитися з вами, як вас звати і яке ваше прізвище?

We can hope for a better future.
My mozhemo spodivatysya na krashche maybutnye.
Ми можемо сподіватися на краще майбутнє.

Good luck!
Schast'y! as
Щасти!

To talk / to speak – Hovoryty Говорити
To help - Dopomahaty Допомагати
To smoke - Palyty Палити
To love - Kokhaty Кохати
I love - Ya kokhayu Я кохаю
Again - Znovu Знову
Russian – Rosiys′kyy Російський
How – Yak Як

I want to learn how to speak perfect Ukrainian.
YA khochu navchytysya hovoryty ideal′no ukrayins′koyu.
Я хочу навчитися говорити ідеально українською.

I don't want to smoke again
Ya ne khochu palyty znovu
Я не хочу палити знову

I want to help
Ya khochu dopomohty
Я хочу допомогти

I love you
Ya tebe kokhayu
Я тебе кохаю

I see you
Ya tebe bachu
Я тебе бачу

I need you
Ty meni potribnyy
Ти мені потрібний

Do you speak Ukrainian or Russian?
Vy rozmovlyayete ukrayins′koyu chy rosiys′koyu?
Ви розмовляєте українською чи російською?

*In Ukrainian, *tebe тебе* is the "direct object pronoun" of the pronoun you.

To read - Chytaty Читати
To write - Pysaty Писати
To teach - Vchyty Вчити
To teach - Navchaty Навчати
To close - Zachynyaty Зачиняти
To choose - Vybyraty Вибирати
Sun - Sontse Сонце
Month - Misyats' Місяць
I talk - Ya govoryu Я говорю
Ukrainian - Ukrayins'kyy Український
Language – Mova Мова

I need this book to learn how to read and write in Ukrainian.
Meni potribna tsya knyha, shchob navchytysya chytaty i pysaty ukrayins'koyu.
Мені потрібна ця книга, щоб навчитися читати і писати українською.

I want to teach English in Ukrainian.
YA khochu vykladaty anhliys'ku ukrayins'koyu.
Я хочу викладати англійську українською.

I want turn on the lights and close the door.
YA khochu vvimknuty svitlo i zachynyty dveri.
Я хочу ввімкнути світло і зачинити двері.

I speak with the boy and the girl in Ukrainian
Ya rozmovlyayu z khlopchykom ta divchynkoyu po ukrayins'ky
Я розмовляю з хлопчиком і дівчинкою по українськи

*In Ukrainian, *mova мова* is "language" in English. The terms "English" and "Ukrainian" cannot be used on their own when referring to a language. The word "language" always comes after the relevant word: "English" / *Anhliys'ka mova Англійська мова*; "Ukrainian" / *Ukrayins'ka mova Українська мова*.

To exchange - Obminyuvaty Обмінювати
Money – Hroshi Гроші
To call - Dzvonyty Дзвонити
Brother - Brat Брат
Dad - Tato Тато
To sit - Sydity Сидіти
Together - Razom Разом
To change - Zminyty Змінити
During - Protyagom Протягом
During - Pid chas Під час
Years - Rik Рік
Sky - Nebo Небо
Sorry - Vybachte Вибачте
Big - Velykyy Великий
Never – Nikoly Ніколи

I am never able to exchange this money at the bank.
YA nikoly ne mozhu obminyaty tsi hroshi v banku.
Я ніколи не можу обміняти ці гроші в банку.

I want to call my brother and my dad today
S'ohodni ya khochu dzvonyty moyomu bratovi i moyemu tatovi
Сьогодні я хочу дзвонити мойому братові і моєму татові

I am sorry.
Vybachte.
Вибачте.

I need to move your cat to another chair
Meni potribno peresadyty vashu kishku na inshe krislo
Мені потрібно пересадити вашу кішку на інше крісло

*This *isn't* a phrase book! The purpose of this book is *solely* to provide you with the tools to create *your own* sentences!

Up - Vhoru Вгору
Down - Vnyz Вниз
Of course - Zvychayno Звичайно
To follow - Sliduvaty Слідувати
New - Novyy Новий
Dog - Pes Пес
Welcome - Laskavo prosymo Ласкаво просимо
Sun – Sontse Сонце
To the – Do До
To return - Povernutysya Повернутися
There isn't – Nemaye Немає
There aren't – Yikh nemaye Їх немає
Excuse me - Vybachte Вибачте
Child -Dytyna Дитина

Excuse me, my child is here as well
Vybachte, moya dytyna tezh tut
Вибачте, моя дитина теж тут

Of course I can come to the theater, and I want to sit together with you and with your sister
Zvychayno, ya mozhu pryyty v teatr, i ya khochu sydity razom z toboyu i tvoyeyu sestroyu
Звичайно, я можу прийти в театр, і я хочу сидіти разом з тобою і твоєю сестрою

If you look under the table, you can see the new rug.
Yakshcho vy zahlyanete pid stil, vy pobachyte novyy kylym.
Якщо ви заглянете під стіл, ви побачите новий килим.

I can see the sky from the window
Ya bachu nebo z vikna
Я бачу небо з вікна

The dog wants to follow me to the store.
Sobaka khoche pity za mnoyu v mahazyn.
Собака хоче піти за мною в магазин.

To allow - Dozvolyty Дозволити
To believe - Viryty Вірити
Morning - Ranok Ранок
Except - Krim Крім
To promise - Obitsyaty Обіцяти
Good night – Nadobranich Надобраніч
Good night – Dobranich Добраніч
To recognize – Vyznaty Визнати
To recognize – Vpiznaty Впізнати
People - Lyudy Люди
Far - Daleko Далеко
Him - Vin Він
His – Yogo Його
Her - Yiyi Її
Police - Politsiya Поліція
Police - Militsiya Міліція

I need to allow him to go with us.
Meni potribno dozvolyty yomu pity z namy.
Мені потрібно дозволити йому піти з нами.

Come here quickly.
Ydy syudy shvydshe.
Йди сюди швидше.

I can't recognize him.
YA ne mozhu yoho vpiznaty.
Я не можу його впізнати.

I believe everything except for this
YA viryu vs′omu, krim ts′oho
Я вірю всьому, крім цього

I want his car
Ya khochu yogo mashynu
Я хочу його машину

Call the police!
Vyklyčte miliciju
Викличте міліцію

Man - Cholovik Чоловік
To live - Zhyty Жити
To enter - VviytyВвійти
To receive - Otrymaty Отримати
To prefer - Viddavaty perevagu Віддавати перевагу
To put - Poklasty Покласти
To move -Rukhatysya Рухатися
To move *(to a place)* -Pereselyatysya Переселятися
Less - Menshe Менше
Each, every – Kozhen Кожен
Good afternoon - Dobryy den′ Добрий день
Afternoon – Poluden 'Полудень
Left - Livoruch Ліворуч
Right - Pravyl′no Правильно
Different - Inshyy Інший
I must - Ya povynen Я повинен

He is a different man now.
Teper vin inshyy cholovik.
Тепер він інший чоловік.

I see the sun in the morning from the kitchen
Ya bachu sontse vrantsi z kukhni
Я бачу сонце вранці з кухні

I want to pay less than you.
YA khochu platyty menshe, nizh ty.
Я хочу платити менше, ніж ти.

I prefer to put this here.
YA vvazhayu za krashche pomistyty tse tut.
Я вважаю за краще помістити це тут.

Where do you live?
De ty zhyvesh?
Де ти живеш?

*With the knowledge you've gained so far, now try to create your own sentences!

To wish - Bazhaty Бажати
Bad - Pohanyy Поганий
To get - Otrymaty Отримати
To forget - Zabuty Забути
Everybody / Everyone - Vsi Всі
Although - Khocha Хоча
Even though - Nezvazhayuchy na Незважаючи на
To feel - Vidchuvaty Відчувати
Great - Chudovyy Чудовий
Great - Velykyy Великий
To like - Podobatys' Подобатись
To like - Lyubyty Юбити
In front - Poperedu Попереду
Past – Mynule Минуле
Through - Cherez Через
Well - Dobre Добре

I don't want to wish anything bad
Ya ne khochu bazhaty nichoho pohanoho
Я не хочу бажати нічого поганого

I must forget everybody from my past.
YA povynen zabuty vsikh zi svoho mynuloho.
Я повинен забути всіх зі свого минулого.

To feel well I must take vitamins
Dlya khoroshoho samopochuttya potribno pryymaty vitaminy
Для хорошого самопочуття потрібно приймати вітаміни

I am close to the person behind you
Ya poruch iz lyudynoyu, yaka stoyit' za vamy
Я поруч із людиною, яка стоїть за вами

I go into the house from the front entrance and not through the yard.
Zakhodzhu v budynok z paradnoho vkhodu, a ne cherez dvir.
Заходжу в будинок з парадного входу, а не через двір.

Next - Nastupnyy Наступний
Next to - Z kumos' З кимось
Behind - Za За
Behind - Pozadu Позаду
Which - Yakyy Який
Restaurant - Restoran Ресторан
Bathroom - Vanna kimnata Ванна кімната
Bathroom - Tualet туалет
Goodbye - Do pobachennya До побачення

Goodbye my friend.
Buvay, druzhe.
Бувай, друже.

Which is the best restaurant in the area?
Yakyy naykrashchyy restoran u ts′omu rayoni?
Який найкращий ресторан у цьому районі?

I can feel the heat.
YA vidchuvayu teplo.
Я відчуваю тепло.

I need to repair a part of the cabinet of the bathroom.
Meni potriben remont chastyny shafy vannoyi kimnaty.
Мені потрібен ремонт частини шафи ванної кімнати.

I want a car before the next year
Ya khochu mashynu na nastupnyy rik
Я хочу машину на наступний рік

I like the house, however it is very small
Meni podobayet′sya budynok, prote vin duzhe malen′kyy
Мені подобається будинок, проте він дуже маленький

*In Ukrainian, whenever "what" is preceded by a noun, you say *yakyy який*. For example: *yakyy який* (m.), *yaka яка* (f.), *yake яке* (n.), *yaki які* (p.)

*In Ukrainian, *z kumos' з кимось* means "next to," for example, "I am next to him." While *nastupnyy наступний* means "the following," for example "the next exit."

To remove - Vydalyty Видалити
To remove - Znyaty зняти
Beautiful - Harnyy Гарний
To lift -Pidnimaty Піднімати
Include / Including - Vklyuchyty Включити
Belong - Nalezhyt' Належить
To check - Pereviryaty Перевіряти
Small - Malen'ka Маленька
Small - Malen'kyy Маленький
So - Tak Так
So - Otzhe Отже

She wants to remove this door
Vona khoche znyaty tsi dveri
Вона хоче зняти ці двері

We need to check the size of the house
Meni potribno pereviryty rozmir budynku
Мені потрібно перевірити розмір будинку

I want to lift this.
YA khochu tse pidnyaty.
Я хочу це підняти.

Can you please put the wood in the fire?
Chy mozhete vy pidklasty drov u vohon'?
Чи можете ви підкласти дров у вогонь?

This doesn't belong here, I need to check again
Tse ne povynno buty tut, meni potribno pereviryty znovu
Це не повинно бути тут, мені потрібно перевірити знову

*In Ukrainian, both *tak так* and *otzhe отже* are used to indicate "so". However *tak так* definition of "so" is used to express cases such as "so much", or "so big." While *otzhe отже* definition of "so" is used to indicate "then."

Please - Bud'laska Будь ласка
Real - Spravzhniy Справжній
Weather – Pohoda Погода
Size - Rozmir Розмір
Doesn't – Ne khoche Не хоче
Price – Tsina Ціна
To hold - Trymaty Тримати
High – Vysokyy Високий
Expensive – Doroho Дорого
Hospital - Likarnya Лікарня

Is that a real diamond?
Tse spravzhniy diamant?
Це справжній діамант?

This week the weather was very beautiful
Na tsyomu tyzhni pohoda bula duzhe harna
На цьому тижні погода була дуже гарна

I can pay this although the price is expensive
Ya mozhu zaplatyty tse, khocha tsina vysoka (dorozhcha).
Я можу заплатити це, хоча ціна висока (дорожча).

Can you please hold my hand?
Vy mozhete potrymaty mene za ruku?
Ви можете потримати мене за руку?

Where is the hospital?
De likarnya?
Де лікарня?

The sun is high in the sky.
Sontse vysoko v nebi.
Сонце високо в небі.

Is everything included in this price?
Chy vse vklyucheno v tsyu tsinu?
Чи все включено в цю ціну?

Building Bridges

In Building Bridges, we take six conjugated verbs that have been selected after studies I have conducted for several months in order to determine which verbs are most commonly conjugated, and which are then automatically followed by an infinitive verb. For example, once you know how to say, "I need," "I want," "I can," and "I like," you will be able to connect words and say almost anything you want more correctly and understandably. The following three pages contain these six conjugated verbs in first, second, third, fourth, and fifth person, as well as some sample sentences.

I want - Ya khochu Я хочу
I need - Meni potribno Мені потрібно
I can - Ya mozhu Я можу
I like - Meni podobayet'sya Мені подобається
I go - Ya idu Я іду
I have to/ I must - Ya povynen Я повинен
To have - U mene ye У мене є
To have - Maty Мати

I want to go to my apartment
Ya khochu ity do moyeyi kvartyry
Я хочу іти до моєї квартири

I can go with you to the bus station
Ya mozhu ity z toboyu na avtovokzal
Я можу іти з тобою на автовокзал

I need to leave the museum.
Meni potribno pokynuty muzey.
Мені потрібно покинути музей.

I like to eat oranges.
YA lyublyu yisty apel'syny.
Я люблю їсти апельсини.

I am want to teach a class
Ya khochu navchaty klas
Я хочу навчати клас

I have to speak to my teacher
Ya povynen rozmovlyaty z moyim vchytelem
Я повинен розмовляти з моїм вчителем

Please master *every* single page up until here prior to attempting the following two pages!

You want - Ty khochesh Ти хочеш

Do you want? - Chy ty khochesh? Чи ти хочеш?

He wants - Vin khoche Він хоче

Does he want? - Chy vin khoche? Чи він хоче?

She wants - Vona khoche Вона хоче

Does she want? - Chy vona khoche? Чи вона хоче?

We want - My khochemo Ми хочемо

Do we want? - Chy my khochemo? Чи ми хочемо?

They want - Vony khochut' Вони хочуть

Do they want? - Chy vony khochut'? Чи вони хочуть?

You (plural) want - Vy khochete Ви хочете

Do you (plural) want - Chy vy khochete? Чи ви хочете?

You need - Tobi potribno Тобі потрібно

Do you need? - Chy tobi potribno? Чи тобі потрібно?

He needs - Yomu potribno Йому потрібно

Does he need? - Chy yomu potribno? Чи йому потрібно?

She needs - Vona potrebuye Вона потребує

Does she need? - Chy vona potrebuye? Чи вона потребує?

We Need - Nam potribno Нам потрібно

Do we need? - Chy nam potribno? Чи нам потрібно?

They need - Yim potribno Їм потрібно

Do they need? - Chy yim potribno? Чи їм потрібно?

You (plural) need - Vam potribno Вам потрібно

Do you (plural) need - Chy vam potribno? Чи Вам потрібно?

You can - Ty mozhesh Ти можеш

Can you? - Chy ty mozhesh? Чи ти можеш?

He can - Vin mozhe Він може

Can he? - Chy vin mozhe? Чи він може?

She can - Vona mozhe Вона може

Can she? - Chy vona mozhe? Чи вона може?

We can - My mozhemo Ми можемо

Can we? - Chy my mozhemo? Чи ми можемо?

They can - Vony mozhut' Вони можуть

Can they? - Chy vony mozhut'? Чи вони можуть?

You (plural) can - Vy mozhete Ви можете

Do you (plural) can? - Chy vy mozhete? Чи ви можете?

You like - Tobi podobaet'sya Тобі подобається

Do you like? - Chy tobi podobaet'sya? Чи тобі подобається?

He likes - Yomu podobaet'sya Йому подобається

Does he like? - Chy yomu podobaet'sya? Чи йому подобається?

She like - Yiy podobaet'sya Їй подобається

Does she like? - Chy yiy podobaet'sya? Чи їй подобається?

We like - Nam podobaet'sya Нам подобається

Do we like? - Chu nam podobaet'sya? Чи нам подобається?

They like - Yim podobaet'sya Їм подобається

Do they like? - Chy yim podobaet'sya? Чи їм подобається?

You (plural) like - Vam podobaet'sya Вам подобається

Do you (plural) like? - Chy vam podobaet'sya? Чи вам подобається?

You go - Ty ydesh Ти йдеш

Do you go? - Chy ty ydesh? Чи ти йдеш?

He goes - Vin yde Він йде

Does he go? - Chy vin yde? Чи він йде?

She goes - Vona yde Вона йде

Does she go? - Chy vona yde? Чи вона йде?

We go - My ydemo Ми йдемо

Do we go? - Chy my ydemo? Чи ми йдемо?

They go - Vony ydut' Вони йдуть

Do they go? - Chy vony ydut'? Чи вони йдуть?

You (plural) go - Vy ydete Ви йдете

Do you (plural) go? - Chy vy ydete? Чи ви йдете?

You must - Ty povynen Ти повинен

Do you have to - Chy ty povynen? Чи ти повинен?

He must - Vin povynen Він повинен

Does he have to - Chy vin povynen? Чи він повинен?

She must - Vona povynna Вона повинна

Does she have to - Chy vona povynna? Чи вона повинна?

We have - My povynni Ми повинні

Do we have to - Chy my povynni? Чи ми повинні?

They must - Vony povynni Вони повинні

Do they have to? - Chy vony povynni? Чи вони повинні?

You (plural) must - Vy povynni Ви повинні

Do you (plural) must? - Chy vy povynni? Чи ви повинні?

You have - Ty mayesh Ти маєш (or) u tebe ye у тебе є

He has - Vin maye Він має (or) u n'oho ye у нього є

She has - Vona maye Вона має (or) u neyi ye у неї є

We have - My mayemo Ми маємо (or) u nas ye у нас є

They have - Vony mayut' Вони мають (or) u nyh ye у них є

You (plural) have - Vy mayete Ви маєте (or) u vas ye у вас є

Do you want to go?
Vy khochete pity?
Ви хочете піти?

Does he want to fly?
Chy khoche vin litaty?
Чи хоче він літати?

We want to swim
My khochemo plavaty
Ми хочемо плавати

Do they want to run?
Chy vony khochut' bigaty?
Чи вони хочуть бігати?

Do you need to clean?
Chy ty povynen prybraty?
Чи ти повинен прибрати?

She needs to sing a song
Vona povynna spivaty pisnyu
Вона повинна співати пісню

We need to travel
My povynni podorozhuvaty
Ми повинні подорожувати

They don't need to fight
Vony ne povynni bytysya
Вони не повинні битися

You (plural) need to save your money.
Vam (**plural**) potribno ekonomyty svoyi hroshi.
Вам (**plural**) потрібно економити свої гроші.

Can you hear me?
Chy ty mene chuyesh?
Чи ти мене чуєш?

He can dance very well
Vin mozhe tantsyuvaty duzhe dobre
Він може танцювати дуже добре

We can go out tonight
My mozhemo pity s'ohodni vvecheri
Ми можемо піти сьогодні ввечері

The fireman can break the door during an emergency.
Pid chas nadzvychaynoyi sytuatsiyi pozhezhnyy mozhe zlamaty dveri.
Під час надзвичайної ситуації пожежний може зламати двері.

Do you like to eat here?
Chy tobi podobayet'sya yisty tut?
Чи тобі подобається їсти тут?

He likes to spend time here
Yomu podobayet'sya provodyty chas tut
Йому подобається проводити час тут

We like to fix the house
Nam podobayet'sya remontuvaty budynok
Нам подобається ремонтувати будинок

They like to cook
Yim podobayet'sya hotuvaty
Їм подобається готувати

You (plural) like to play soccer.
Vy (**plural**) lyubyte hraty u futbol.
Ви (**plural**) любите грати у футбол.

Do you go to the movies on weekends?
Chy vy khodyte v kino na vykhidnykh?
Чи ви ходите в кіно на вихідних?

He goes fishing
Vin yde lovyty rybu
Він йде ловити рибу

We are going to relax
My ydemo vidpochyvaty
Ми йдемо відпочивати

They go out to eat at a restaurant every day.
Vony shchodnya ydutʹ poyisty v restoran.
Вони щодня йдуть поїсти в ресторан.

Do you have money?
Chy ty mayesh hroshi?
Чи ти маєш гроші?

She must look outside
Vona povynna vyhlyanuty nazovni
Вона повинна виглянути назовні

We have to sign here
My povynni pidpysaty tut
Ми повинні підписати тут

They have to send the letter
Vony povynni vidpravyty lysta
Вони повинні відправити листа

You (plural) have to stand in line.
Vy (**plural**) povynni stoyaty v cherzi.
Ви (**plural**) повинні стояти в черзі.

Other Useful Tools in the Ukrainian Language

Days of the Week
Sunday - Nedilya Неділя
Monday - Ponedilok Понеділок
Tuesday - Vivtorok Вівторок
Wednesday - Sereda Середа
Thursday - Chetver Четвер
Friday - Pyatnytsya Пятниця
Saturday – Subota Субота

Months of the year
January - Sichyen Січень
February - Lyotiy Лютий
March - Byeryezyen Березень
April - Kvityen Квітень
May - Travyen Травень
June - Chyervyen Червень
July - Lipyen Липень
August - Syerpyen Серпень
September - Vyeryesyen Вересень
October - Zovtyen Жовтень
November - Listopad Листопад
December - Guroodyen Грудень

Seasons
Spring - Vesna Весна
Summer - Lito Літо
Autumn - Osin' Осінь
Winter – Zyma Зима

Cardinal Directions
North - Pivnich Північ
South - Pivden' Південь
East - Skhid Схід
West – Zakhid Захід

Colors
Black - Chornyy Чорний
White - Bilyy Білий
Gray - Siryy Сірий
Red - Chervonyy Червоний
Blue - Syniy Синій
Yellow - Zhovtyy Жовтий
Green - Zelenyy Зелений
Orange - Pomaranchevyy Помаранчевий
Purple - Fioletovyy Фіолетовий
Brown – Korychnevyy Коричневий

Numbers
One - Odyn Один
Two - Dva Два
Three - Try Три
Four - Chotyry Чотири
Five - P'yat' П'ять
Six - Shist' Шість
Seven - Sim Сім
Eight - Visim Вісім
Nine - Dev'yat' Дев'ять
Ten - Desyat' Десять

Conversational Bulgarian Quick and Easy
The Most Innovative Technique to Learn the Bulgarian Language

YATIR NITZANY

The Bulgarian Language

Bulgarian is an Indo-European language and a member of the southern branch of the Slavic language family. It uses a Cyrillic alphabet and is spoken by over 8 million people mainly in Bulgaria, but also in Ukraine, Macedonia, Serbia, Turkey, Greece, Romania, Canada, USA, Australia, Germany, and Spain. Bulgarian is mutually intelligible with Macedonian, and fairly closely related to Serbian, Croatian, Bosnian, and Slovenian.

With the accession of Bulgaria to the European Union in 2007, Bulgarian is now also one of the official languages of the European Union.

Modern Bulgarian dates from the 16th century onwards and it underwent general grammar and syntax changes in the 18th and 19th centuries. Present-day written Bulgarian language was standardized after Bulgaria became independent in 1878 on the basis of the 19th-century Bulgarian vernacular. Many Turkish words were adopted into Bulgarian during the long period of Ottoman rule. Words have also been borrowed from Latin, Greek, Russian, French, Italian, German, and increasingly from English.

The Program

Memorize the vocabulary:

I - Az Аз
I am - Az sŭm Аз съм
With you - S teb С теб
With us – S nas С нас
For you - Za teb За теб
For you - (**Plural**) Za vas За вас
Are you - Ti li si Ти ли си
You are - Ti si Ти си
You - Ti Ти
You (plural) - Vie Вие
From - Ot От

Sentences composed from the vocabulary you just learned

I am from Bulgaria
Az sŭm ot Bŭlgariya
Аз съм от България

Are you from Sofia?
Ti ot Sofiya li si?
Ти от София ли си?

I am with you
Az sŭm s teb/vas (p)
Аз съм с теб/вас

This is for you
Tova e za teb/vas (p)
Това е за теб/вас

*Az sum is pronounced [az səm]

*Bulgarian nouns have the categories grammatical gender, number, case (only vocative), and definiteness. A noun has one of three specific grammatical genders (masculine, feminine, neuter) and two numbers (singular and plural).

With him - S nego С него
With her - S neya С нея
Without him - Bez nego Без него
Always - Vinagi Винаги
Is - E Е
It is - Tova e това е
Sometimes - Ponyakoga Понякога
Today – Dnes Днес

Are you at the house?
v kŭshtata li si
в къщата ли си

I am always with her
Vinagi sŭm s neya
Винаги съм с нея

Are you alone today?
Sam li si dnes
сам ли си днес

Sometimes I go without him.
Ponyakoga hodya/otivam bez nego.
Понякога ходя/отивам без него.

I am there with him
Az sŭm tam s nego
Аз съм там с него

*In Bulgarian you don't always use the full form "it's" / *tova e*, but just "is" /*e*.

*In Bulgarian if the question doesn't have the question word: where, who, what, how, etc., you have to put the question particle *li*- Ли after the preposition, or the verb. It always goes together with the relevant auxiliary verb, for example: *ti vie*. In the question, "**Are you alone today**?" you have to insert the particle *li* between "them" and "today" and to put after it *si*, which is the auxiliary verb for "you" - *ti* - *Ti bez tyah **li si** dnes*? Ти без тях ли си днес ? The word *li* does not mean anything by itself. It is only used to form questions.

107

Was – Beshe byah Беше бях
I was - Byah Бях
To be - Da bŭdesh Да бъдеш
Here - Tuk Тук
Very - Mnogo Много
And - Ee И
Between - Mezhdu Между
If - Ako Ако
Now - Sega Сега
Tomorrow - Utre Утре
Where - Kŭde Къде
Where are you from? - Ot kŭde si? От къде си?
How are you? - Kak si? Как си?
Without them - Bez tyakh Без тях
This - Tova Това
There - Tam Там
He - Toĭ Той
She - Tya тя

I was here with them
Byakh tuk s tyakh
Бях тук с тях

I was home at 5pm
Byakh si vkŭshti v 17 chasa
Бях си вкъщи в 17 часа

Between now and tomorrow.
Mezhdu sega i utre.
Между сега и утре.

Where are you from?
Ot kŭde si?
От къде си?

You and I
Az i ti
Аз и ти

Later - Po-kŭsno По-късно
Later - Posle После
After - Sled След
Afterwards - Sled tova След това
Yes - Da Да
To – Za За
To – Da Да
Happy - Shtastliv Щастлив
Better - Po-dobre По-добре
Day - Den' Ден
Then - Sled tova След това
Then - Togava тогава
Good morning - Dobro utro Добро утро
How old are you? - Na kolko godini si? На колко години си?
Good - Dobre Добре
Same - Sŭshtoto Същото

It's better to be home later.
Po-dobre e da si vkŭshti po-kŭsno/posle.
По-добре е да си вкъщи по-късно/после.

If this is good, then I am happy.
Ako tova e dobre, znachi sŭm shtastliv.
Ако това е добре, значи съм щастлив.

Yes, you are very good
Da, mnogo si dobŭr
Да, много си добър

Good morning, how are you today?
Dobro utro, kak si dnes?
Добро утро, как си днес?

How old are you?
Na kolko godini si?
На колко години си?

Okay – Dobre Добре
Okay – Okey Окей
Everything - Vsichko Всичко
Somewhere - Nyakŭde Някъде
Maybe - Mozhe bi Може би
What - Kakvo Какво
Almost - Pochti Почти
I go - Otivam Отивам
Worse - Po-losho По-лошо
Even if - Dori ako Дори ако
No - Ne Не

This is for us.
Tova e za nas.
Това е за нас.

Even if I go now
Dori da/ako otida sega
Дори да/ако отида сега

What? I am almost there
Kakvo? pochti stignakh
Какво? почти стигнах

Where are you?
Kŭde si?
Къде си?

Where is everything?
Kŭde e vsichko
Къде е всичко

Maybe somewhere
Mozhe bi nyakŭde
Може би някъде

*The definitive of "same" (*sashto*) is *sash**toto*** (N), or *sash**tiat*** (M)/ *sush**tata*** (F). As you can see, it is affected by the gender and the ending of the word, and is different for the different ones.

Already - Veche Вече
Son - Sin Син
Daughter - Dŭshterya Дъщеря
Hard – Tvŭrd Твърд
Hard (as in difficult) - Trudno Труден
Still - Vse pak Все пак
Impossible - Nevŭzmozhno Невъзможно
House - Kŭshta Къща
Home - Dom Дом
In / at – V В
In / at – Na НА
Car - Avtomobil Автомобил
Car - Kolà Кола
Book - Kniga Книга
Isn't – Ne e Не е

She is not in the car, so maybe she is still at the house?
Tya ne e v kolata, taka che mozhe bi vse oshte e v kŭshtata?
Тя не е в колата, така че може би все още е в къщата?

I am already in the car with your son and daughter
Veche sŭm v kolata sŭs sina i dŭshterya vi
Вече съм в колата със сина и дъщеря ви

This is very hard, but it's not impossible
Tova e mnogo trudno, no ne e nevŭzmozhno
Това е много трудно, но не е

*Used definitive form. The word "book" – *kniga* in Bulgarian is a feminine one, and gets its definite form by adding the suffix -ta, *knigata*.

*In Bulgarain "s" becomes "sŭs" (СЪС) in case the following word begins with the letters S or Z. Same rule applies for "in" – "v" - "В". V/B becomes Vŭv (ВЪВ) in case the following wr begins with V or F. For example: With me: "s men" - С мен / "with Sarah" sŭs Sara -Със Сара / "in the bedroom" v spalnyata - в спалнята / in Vienna: vŭv Viena - Във Виена.

Thank you - Blagodarya Благодаря
Please - Molya Моля
For - Za За
That - Tova Това
This is - Tova e Това е
But - No Но
However - Vŭpreki tova Въпреки това
No / not - Ne Не
I am not - Ne sŭm Не съм
Away - Dalech Далеч
Similar - Podobni Подобни
Our / ours - Nashata Нашата
Doesn't - Ne Не
Embassy - Posolstvo Посолство

Thank you, Kenneth.
Blagodarya ti, Kenet.
Благодаря ти, Кенет.

I am not here, I am far away
Ne sŭm tuk, daleche sŭm
Не съм тук, далече съм

That house is similar to ours.
Kŭshtata e podobna na nashata.
Къщата е подобна на нашата.

One moment please!
Yedin momyent, molya!
Един момент, моля!

What is this?
Kakvo ye tova?
Какво е това?

Where is the American embassy?
Kŭde e amerikanskoto posolstvo?
Къде е американското посолство?

I say / I am saying - Kazvam Казвам
What time is it? - Kolko e chasŭt? Колко е часът?
I want - Iskam Искам
Without you - Bez teb Без теб
Everywhere - Navsyakŭde Навсякъде
Wherever - Kŭdeto i da e Където и да е
I go / I am going - Otivam Отивам
I am not going - Az nyama da otida Аз няма да отида
Light - Svetlina Светлина
I need - Imam nuzhda Имам нужда
I must - Tryabva трябва
I see / I am seeing - Vizhdam Виждам
Right now - Tochno sega Точно сега
With - S С

I am saying no / I say no
Kazvam ne
Казвам не

You need to be at home.
Tryabva da si u doma/vkŭsti.
Трябва да си у дома/вкъщи.

I see light outside
Vizhdam svetlina otvŭn
Виждам светлина отвън

What time is it right now?
kolko e chasŭt v momenta?
колко е часът в момента?

I see this everywhere
Vizhdam tova navsyakŭde
Виждам това навсякъде

*This *isn't* a phrase book! The purpose of this book is *solely* to provide you with the tools to create *your own* sentences!

The - (see footnote)
A - (see footnote)
To see – Da vidiya Да видя
Outside - Otvŭn Отвън
Other / Another - Drug Друг
Side - Strana Страна
Until - Do До
Yesterday - Vchera Вчера
Without us - Bez nas Без нас
Day - Den Ден
Before - Predi Преди
Late - Kŭsen Късен
Since - Tŭĭ kato /Тъй като

I am from the other side
Az sŭm ot drugata strana
Аз съм от другата страна

Since the other day
Ot onzi den
От онзи ден

But I was here until late yesterday
No byakh tuk do kŭsno vchera
Но бях тук до късно вчера

The same day
Sŭshtiyat den
Същият ден

*In Bulgarian the article "a" doesn't exist.

*In Bulgarian, the definite article "the" doesn't exist as a separate word but as a suffix. Because it's a word suffix, the definite article is also affected by the gender and ending of the word, and is different for different ones: *–yat* and *–ya* for masculine gender (E.g. "the same day"/ *sashtiyat den*) /*–ta* for feminine gender (E.g. "the good book" / *dobrata kniga*) / *–to* for neuter gender (E.g. "the good child"/ *dobroto dete*) / *–te* for plural (E.g. "the good people"/ *dobrite hora*).

Easy - Lesno Лесно
To find - Namiram Намирам
To look for / to search - Da tŭrsish Да търсиш
To wait - Chakam Чакам
To sell - Prodavam Продавам
To use - Izpolzvam Използвам
Night - Nosht Нощ
To decide - Reshavam Решавам

This place is easy to find
Tova myasto e lesno za namirane
Това място е лесно за намиране

I am saying to wait until tomorrow
Kazvam da izchakame do utre
Казвам да изчакаме до утре

It's easy to sell this table
Lesno e da prodadete tazi masa
Лесно е да продадете тази маса

I want to use this
Iskam da izpolzvam tova
Искам да използвам това

Where is the book?
Kŭde e knigata?
Къде е книгата?

I need to decide between both places
Tryabva da resha mezhdu dvete mesta
Трябва да реша между двете места

Is it possible to look for this book in the library.
Vŭzmozhno li e da potŭrsya tazi kniga v bibliotekata.
Възможно ли е да потърся тази книга в библиотеката.

I need to be there at night
Tryabva da sŭm tam prez noshtta
Трябва да съм там през нощта

Tryabva means both "need" and "must;" both will be used interchangeably in this program.

Place - Myasto Място
Because - Zashtoto Защото
Them - Tyakh Тях
They - Te Те
Their - Tekhen Техен
Mine - Moe Мое
Myself - Sebe si Себе си
To understand - Razbiram Разбирам
Problem - Problem Проблем
Problems – Problemi Проблеми
I do / I am doing - Pravya Правя
Of - Na На
To look - Gledam Гледам
To do - Pravya Правя
Near / Close - Blizo Близо

Is this place near?
Tova myasto blizo li e?
Това място близо ли е?

I do what I want.
Pravya kakvoto iskam.
Правя каквото искам.

That book is mine
Tazi kniga e moya
Тази книга е моя

I need to understand the problem
Tryabva da razbera problema
Трябва да разбера проблема

*Used definitive forms. The word "house" – *kashta* is a feminine one, and gets its definite form by adding -*ta*, *kashta**ta**.

*With the knowledge you've gained so far, now try to create your own sentences!

Enough - Stiga Стига
Enough - Dostatŭchno достатъчно
To buy - Kupuvam Купувам
Food - hrana Храна
Water - Voda Вода
Hotel - Hotel Хотел
Both - I dvete И двете
Like this - Go taka Го така
That's why - Eto zashto Ето защо
To have - Imam Имам

I like this hotel because it's near the beach
Kharesvam tozi khotel, zashtoto e blizo do plazha
Харесвам този хотел, защото е близо до плажа

I want to look at the view.
Iskam da pogledna gledkata.
Искам да погледна гледката.

I want to buy a bottle of water
Iskam da si kupya butilka voda
Искам да си купя бутилка вода

Do it like this!
Napravi go taka!
Направи го така!

I have a view of the city from the hotel.
Imam gledka kŭm grada ot khotela.
Имам гледка към града от хотела.

Both of them have enough food
I dvamata imat dostatŭchno khrana
И двамата имат достатъчно храна

*Nouns in the Bulgarian language are split into three categories gender, number, case, and definiteness. Each and every noun has one of these specific grammatical genders of either neuter, masculine, or feminine and usually two numbers of either plural or singular.

I like - haresvam Харесвам
Family - Semeĭstvo Семейство
Parents - Roditeli Родители
Why - Zashto Защо
To say - kazvam казвам
Something - Neshto Нещо
To go - Da otida Да отида
To work - Rabotya Работя
Who - Koĭ Кой
Important - Vazhno Важно
What is your name? - Kak se kazvash? Как се казваш?
Your - Tvoyat Твоят (when used for "you" singular form)
Your - Vashiyat Вашият (formal or plural)
Hi – Zdrasti Здрасти
Hello - Zdraveĭte Здравейте

Hello, what is your name?
Zdraveĭ kak se kazvash?
Здравей как се казваш?

I like to be at home with my parents
Obicham da sŭm vkŭshti s roditelite si
Обичам да съм вкъщи с родителите си

Why do I need to say something important?
Zashto tryabva da kazvam neshto vazhno?
Защо трябва да казвам нещо важно?

I like to work
obicham da rabotya
обичам да работя

Who is there?
Koĭ e tam?
Кой е там?

*In Bulgarian "hello" when used to greet only one person is Zdravey Здравей (while Zdraveyte mentioned above is more formal, or used for cases of more than one person).

To know - Znam Знам
To know - Znaya Зная
There is / There are - Ima Има
Ready - Gotov Готов (singular)
Ready - Gotovi Готови (plural)
Soon - Skoro Скоро
That - (*conjunction*) Che Че
Busy – Zaet Зает
Sun - Slŭntse Слънце

I am busy, but I need to be ready soon
Zaet sŭm, no tryabva da sŭm gotov skoro
Зает съм, но трябва да съм готов скоро

I want to know if they are here.
Iskam da znam dali sa tuk.
Искам да знам дали са тук.

I can go outside.
Moga da izlyaza navŭn.
Мога да изляза навън.

There are seven dolls
Ima sedem kukli
Има седем кукли

There is sun outside today.
Dnes navŭn ima slŭntse.
Днес навън има слънце.

I need to know that everything is ok
Tryabva da znam, che vsichko e nared
Трябва да знам, че всичко е наред

*In the last sentence, "that" is used as a conjunction, *che* че.

*(*Az*) *haresvam* meaning "I like" (Аз) харесвам is a lighter form to express your love for something. When you want to express your deep personal and intimate love for something very close to you, like your home and parents, it's more appropriate to use the word in Bulgarian for "Love" / *Obicham*.

How much - Kolko Колко
To bring - Nosya Нося
With me - S men При мен
Only - Samo Само
When - Koga Кога
I can - Moga Мога
Can I? - Moga li? Мога ли?
Were - Bili Били
Without me - Bez men Без мен

I can work today
Moga da rabotya dnes
Мога да работя днес

Only when you can.
Samo kogato mozhesh.
Само когато можеш.

Go there without me.
Otidete tam bez men.
Отидете там без мен.

How much money do I need to bring with me?
Kolko pari tryabva da nosya sŭs sebe si?
Колко пари трябва да нося със себе си?

Our house is on the mountain.
Nashata kŭshta e v planinata.
Нашата къща е в планината.

*There are three grammatical genders in Bulgarian: masculine (M), feminine (F) and neuter (N). The gender can be determined by the noun's ending: all nouns which ending in a consonant usually are masculiune (for example, *grad* – "city," *sin* – "son", *mazh* – "man"). However, nouns ending in –*a*/–*ya*, like *zhena* – "woman," *dashterya* – "daughter," usually are feminine. Any nouns which end end in –*e*, –*o* usually are neuter *dete* – "child," *ezero* – "lake".

Fast - Bŭrzo Бързо
Slow - Bavno Бавно
Cold - Studeno Студено
Instead - Vmesto tova Вместо това
Inside - Vŭtre Вътре
To eat – Yam Ям
To eat – Za yadene За ядене
Hot - Goreshto Горещо
To Drive – Karam Карам (verb)
To Drive – Da kara Да кара
Cousin - Bratovched Братовчед
Without - Bez Без
Or - Ili Или
Lunch - Obyad Обяд
Bread - Khlyab Хляб
Rice - Oriz Ориз

I like to eat bread instead of rice.
Obicham da yam khlyab vmesto oriz.
Обичам да ям хляб вместо ориз.

I need to drive the car very fast or very slowly.
Трябва да карам колата много бързо или много бавно.
Tryabva da karam kolata mnogo bŭrzo ili mnogo bavno.

It is cold in the library.
V bibliotekata e studeno.
В библиотеката е студено.

I like to eat a hot meal for my lunch.
Obicham da yam topla khrana za obyad.
Обичам да ям топла храна за обяд.

I am happy without any of my cousins here
Shtastliv sŭm bez nikoy ot bratovchedite mi tuk
Щастлив съм без никои от братовчедите ми тук

To answer - Otgovaryam Отговарям
To fly – Letya Летя
How - Kak Как
Many /much /a lot - Mnogo Много
I go to - Otivam do Отивам до
World – Svyat Свят
Church - Tsŭrkva Църква
Around - Naokolo Наоколо
Yours - Tvoĭ Твой
To walk - Vŭrvya Вървя
Children - Detsa Деца
School - Uchilishte Училище
Question - Vŭpros Въпрос
English - Angliĭski Английски

The children are yours
Detsata sa tvoi
Децата са твои

I need to answer many questions.
Tryabva da otgovorya na mnogo vŭprosi.
Трябва да отговоря на много въпроси.

I want to fly today.
Iskam da letya dnes.
Искам да летя днес.

You need to walk around the school.
Tryabva da se razkhodite iz uchilishteto.
Трябва да се разходите из училището.

Where is the Church?
Kŭde e Tsŭrkvata?
Къде е Църквата?

Do you speak English?
Govorite li anglijski
Говорите ли английски

To swim - Pluvam Плувам
To practice - Praktikuvam Практикувам
To play - Igraya Играя
To leave - (to leave something) Ostavya Оставя
Better - Po-dobre По-добре
To travel - Pŭtuvam Пътувам
To learn - Ucha Уча

I want to leave my dog at home.
Iskam da ostavya kucheto si u doma.
Искам да оставя кучето си у дома.

I want to travel the world.
Iskam da pŭtuvam po sveta.
Искам да пътувам по света.

I need to learn to swim.
Tryabva da se naucha da pluvam.
Трябва да се науча да плувам.

I want to learn how to play better tennis.
Iskam da se naucha da igraya po-dobre tenis.
Искам да се науча да играя по-добре тенис.

*In Bulgarian there are three genders (as in Russian or German): masculine (*mazhki rod*), feminine (*zhenski rod*) and neuter (*sreden rod*). Every word has a gender and there are some rules for their determinations: Masculine words end usually in a consonant, or in *iy*: *mazh* / "a man," *valk* / "a wolf," *film*/ "a film," *geroiy*/ "a hero," *zhivot* / "a life". But there are some words that end in –*A* or –*O*: *bashta* / "a father," *chicho*/ "an uncle," *dyado* / "a grandfather," *sadia*/ "a judge," etc. Feminine words end usually in –*A*, –*Ya*, –*Ost*, –*Est*: *zhena*/ "a woman," *masa*/ "a table," *kashta*/ "a house," *yabalka*/ "an apple," *staya*/ "a room," *radost*/ "joy," *bolest* / "an illness," etc. There are a few exceptions that end in a consonant: *nosht* / "a night," *krav* / "blood," *zahar* / "sugar," *sol* / "salt," *esen* / "autumn," etc. The nouns that belong to the neuter gender have endings –*O*, –*E*, or end in *E, I, U, Yu*(the latter are usually loan words): *momche* / "a boy," *momiche* / "a girl," *ezero* / "a lake," *litse* / "a face," *ime* / "a name" *taksi* / "a taxi," *bizhu* / "a jewel," *menyu* / "a menu".

Against - Protiv Против
Us - Nie Ние
To visit - poseshtavam Посещавам
Mom - Mama Мама
Mother - Maĭka Майка
To give - davam давам
Just - Prosto Просто
Week - Sedmitsa Седмица
Than - Otkolkoto Отколкото
Nothing - Nishto Нищо
Anything - Vsichko Всичко
Anything - Kakvoto i da e Каквото и да е
Each / Every - Vseki Всеки

Something is better than nothing
Neshto e po-dobro ot nishto
Нещо е по-добро от нищо.

I am against him
Az sŭm protiv nego
Аз съм против него

You do this every day?
Pravite tova vseki den?
Правите това всеки ден?

We go to visit my family each week.
Poseshtavame semeĭstvoto mi vsyaka sedmitsa.
Посещаваме семейството ми всяка седмица.

I need to give you something
Tryabva da ti dam neshto
Трябва да ти дам нещо

*In Bulgarian, *ti* / "ти: is the indirect object pronouns of the pronoun "you," the person who is actually affected by the action that is being carried out. *I need to give you something* - "Tryabva da **ti** dam neshto" - "Трябва да **ти** дам нещо".

Towards - Kŭm Към
To meet - Sreshtam Срещам
Someone - Nyakoĭ Някой
Wednesday – Sryada Сряда
To drink - Piya Пия
Woman - Zhena Жена
To begin / to start - Zapochvam Започвам
To finish - Priklyuchvam Приключвам
To help - Pomagam Помагам
In order to – Za da За да
Good afternoon - Dobŭr den Добър ден
Afternoon – Sledobed Следобед
Evening – Vecher Вечір

Do you want to meet someone?
iskash li da se zapoznaesh s nyakogo
искаш ли да се запознаеш с някого

I am here on Wednesdays.
Tuk sŭm i v sryada.
Тук съм и в сряда.

We want to start the class soon.
Iskame da zapochnem chasovete skoro.
Искаме да започнем часовете скоро.

In order to finish at three o'clock this afternoon, I need to finish soon
Za da priklyucha v tri chasa tozi sledobed, tryabva da svŭrsha skoro
За да приключа в три часа този следобед, трябва да свърша скоро

*In Bulgarian, if it is about the time before 10 p.m. you should say *vecher* / "evening;" if it is after 10 p.m. - *nosht* / "night."

*In Bulgarian, the plurals of the names of the days are formed with the suffix –ite: *Ponedelnik – Ponedelnicite*; *Vtornicite*; *Sryadite*; *Chetvartacite*; *Petacite; Sabotite; Nedelite*;

I have - Imam Имам
Don't - Nedeĭ Недей
Friend - Priyatel Приятел
To borrow - Vemam na zaem Вземам на заем
To borrow - Zaemam Заемам
Grandfather - Dyado Дядо
To want – Iskam Искам
To stay - ostavam Оставам
Way - Pŭt Път
Nobody / anyone - Nikoĭ Никой
My - Moi Мой (see footnote)
My - Moya Моя (see footnote)

I want to borrow this book for my grandfather
Iskam da zaema tazi kniga za dyado mi
Искам да заема тази книга за дядо ми

Why don't you have the book?
Zashto nyamash knigata?
Защо нямаш книгата?

I want to stay in Sofia because I have a friend there.
Iskam da ostana v Sofiya, zashtoto imam priyatel tam.
Искам да остана в София, защото имам приятел там.

*In the Bulgarian language, in relation to gender, the pronouns will have different conjugations:

- "her" / *neyno*, his/ *negovo*/ *negov*, its/ *negovo*, he/ *toi*, she/ *tya*, it/ *to*, they / *te*

- "my" / *moi* (male), *moya* (female), *moe* (neutral), *moite* (plural)

- "their" / *tehen* (male), *tyahna* (female), *tyahno* (neutral), *tehnite* (plural)

- "your" / *tvoy* (male), *tvoya* (female), *tvoe* (neutral), *tvoite* (plural)

- "your" (singular formal or plural)/ *vash* (male), *vasha* (fem), *vashe* (neuter), *vashi* (plural)

- "our" / *nash* (male), *nasha* (female), *nashe* (neutral), *nashi* (plural)

To look like - Da izglezhda kato Да изглежда като
To show - Pokazvam Показвам
To prepare - Prigotvyam Приготвям
I don't - Ne
Do you want? - Iskash li Искаш ли
About - Otnosno Относно
Time - (see footnote)
First – Pŭrvo Първо
First time - Pŭrvi pŭt Първи път

Do you want to look like Arnold
Iskash li da izlezhdash kato Arnold
Искаш ли да изглеждаш като Арнолд

I don't want to see anyone here
Ne iskam da vizhdam nikogo tuk
Не искам да виждам никого тук

I need to show you how to prepare breakfast
Tryabva da ti pokazha kak se prigotvya zakuska
Трябва да ти покажа как се приготвя закуска

That is incorrect, I don't need the car today
Tova ne e vyarno, nyamam nuzhda ot kolata dnes
Това не е вярно, нямам нужда от колата днес

Since the first time
Ot pŭrviya pŭt
От първия път

We are here for a long time
Tuk sme ot dosta vreme
Тук сме от доста време

*In Bulgarian there are 3 definitions for "time":
Time - Chas Час (reference to; hour, "what time is it?")
Time - Vreme Време (era, moment period, duration of time)
Time – Pŭt Път (occasion or frequency) and the plural form is pŭti пъти.

To remember – Pomnya Помня
To remember – Zapomnyam Запомням
Number - Nomer Номер
Hour - Chas Час
Dark - Tŭmno Тъмно
Darkness - Mrak Мрак
Grandmother - Baba Баба
Five - Pet Пет
Minute - Minuta Минута
Minutes - Minuti Минути
More - Oshte Още
To think - Mislya Мисля
To hear - Chuvam Чувам
Last - Posledno Последно
To come - Idvam Идвам

I want to come with you.
iskam da doĭda s teb
искам да дойда с теб

I need to remember your number
Tryabva da zapomnya nomera ti
Трябва да запомня номера ти

This is the last hour of darkness
Tova e posledniyat chas na tŭmninata
Това е последният час на тъмнината

I can hear my grandmother speaking Bulgarian.
Chuvam baba mi da govori bŭlgarski.
Чувам баба ми да говори български.

I need to think about this more.
Tryabva da pomislya poveche za tova.
Трябва да помисля повече за това.

From here to there, it's only five minutes
Ot tuk do tam sa samo pet minuti
От тук до там са само пет минути

Again - Otnovo Отново
To take - Vzemam Вземам
To try - Probvam Пробвам
To rent - Naemam Наемам
To happen - Da se sluchi Да се случи
Without her - Bez neya Без нея
To turn off - Izklyuchvam Изключвам
To turn on - Vklyuchvam Включвам
To ask – Da popitam Да попитам
To ask – Pitam Питам
To stop - Spiram Спирам
Early - Rano Рано
Beach – Plazh Плаж
Tonight - Tazi vecher Тази вечер
Why - Zashto Защо
Sad – Tŭzhen Тъжен

He must go and rent a house at the beach.
Toĭ tryabva da otide i da naeme kŭshta na plazha.
Той трябва да отиде и да наеме къща на плажа.

I need to turn off the lights early tonight
Tazi vecher tryabva da izgasya svetlinite rano
Тази вечер трябва да изгася светлините рано

We want to stop here
Iskame da sprem tuk
Искаме да спрем тук

This needs to happen today.
Tova tryabva da se sluchi dnes.
Това трябва да се случи днес.

Why are you sad right now?
Zashto si tŭzhen sega?
Защо си тъжен сега?

*Sad = *tazhen* (M), *tazhna* (F), *tazhno* (N), *tazhni* (Plural)

To order - Porŭchvam Поръчвам
Permission - Razreshenie Разрешение
Building - Sgrada Сграда
Doctor - Lekar Лекар
Exact - Tochno Точно
To leave - (to leave a place) Napuskam Напускам
In order to – Za За
Airport - Letishteto Летището
Bulgaria - Bŭlgariya България
We are - Nie sme Ние сме

I want to order a soup.
Iskam da porŭcham supa.
Искам да поръчам супа.

We are from America
Nie sme ot Amerika
Ние сме от Америка

Your doctor is in the same building.
Vashiyat lekar e v sŭshtata sgrada.
Вашият лекар е в същата сграда.

In order to leave you have to ask permission.
Za da napusnete, tryabva da poiskate razreshenie.
За да напуснете, трябва да поискате разрешение.

Is it possible to know the exact date?
Vŭzmozhno li e da se znae tochnata data?
Възможно ли е да се знае точната дата?

Where is the airport?
Kŭde e letishteto?
Къде е летището?

I want to go to sleep
iskam da si lyagam
искам да си лягам

To open - Otvaryam Отварям
To pay - Plashtam Плащам
To buy - Kupuvam Купувам
To hope - Nadyavam se Надявам се
A bit, a little, a little bit - Malko Малко
Sister - Sestra Сестра
Name - Ime Име
Last name - Familiya Фамилия
Door - Vrata Врата
Future - Bŭdeshte Бъдеще
Nice to meet you - Radvam se da se zapoznaem
Радвам се да се запознаем

I need to open the door for my sister
Tryabva da otvorya vratata na sestra mi
Трябва да отворя вратата на сестра ми

I need to buy something
Tryabva da kupya neshto
Трябва да купя нещо

I want to meet your brothers.
Iskam da se zapoznaya s bratyata ti.
Искам да се запозная с братята ти.

Nice to meet you, what is your name and your last name?
Radvam se da se zapoznaem, kak sa dvete ti imena i?
Радвам се да се запознаем, как са двете ти имена ?

We can hope for a better future.
Mozhem da se nadyavame na po-dobro bŭdeshte.
Можем да се надяваме на по-добро бъдеще.

*As previously stated, in Bulgarian, the definite article "the" doesn't exist as a separate word but as a suffix to the words. You should add the suffix *-ŭt*, when the noun is a subject in the sentence, and as *–a*, when the word is not. In the case of our sentence, we translate "the mall" as *mol-a*.

To talk / to speak - Govorya Говоря
To help - Pomogna Помогна
To smoke - Pusha Пуша
To love - Obicham Обичам
I love - Obicham Обичам
Again - Otnovo Отново
Bulgarian - Bŭlgarski Български
Perfect - Perfekten Перфектен

I want to learn how to speak perfect Bulgarian.
Iskam da se naucha da govorya perfektno nemski.
Искам да се науча да говоря перфектен български.

I don't want to smoke again
Ne iskam da pusha otnovo
Не искам да пуша отново

I want to help
iskam da pomogna
искам да помогна

I love you
Obicham te
Обичам те

I see you
vizhdam te
виждам те

I need you
nuzhdaya se ot teb
нуждая се от теб

I don't speak Bulgarian very well
Ne govorya balgarski mnogo dobre
Не говоря български много добре

Ot teb is the direct object pronoun of the pronoun "you."

To read - Cheta Чета
To write - Pisha Пиша
To teach - Prepodavam Преподавам
To close - Zatvaryam Затварям
To choose – Izbiram Избирам
To turn on - Vklyuchvam Включвам
Month - Mesets Месец
I talk - Govorya Говоря
Language – Ezik Език
Boy - Momche Момче
Girl - Momiche Момиче

I need this book to learn how to read and write in Bulgarian.
Tazi kniga mi tryabva, za da se naucha da cheta i pisha na bŭlgarski.
Тази книга ми трябва, за да се науча да чета и пиша на български.

I want to teach English in Bulgaria
Iskam da prepodavam angliĭski ezik v Bŭlgariya
Искам да преподавам английски език в България

I want turn on the lights and close the door.
Iskam da zapalya lampite i da zatvorya vratata.
Искам да запаля лампите и да затворя вратата.

I speak with the boy and the girl in Bulgarian.
govrya na bŭlgarski S momcheto i momicheto
говоря на български с момчето и момичето

I don't understand
Ne razbiram
Не разбирам

I do not know
Ne znam
Не знам

To exchange - Razmenyam разменям
Money – Pari Пари
To call - Obazhdam se обаждам се
Brother - Brat Брат
Dad – Tatko Татко
Dad – Bashta Баща
To sit - Syadam сядам
Together - Zaedno Заедно
To change - Smenyam сменям
To change - Preoblichamse преобличам се (changing clothes)
During - Po vreme na По време на
Years - Godini Години
Sky - Nebe небе
Sorry - Sŭzhalyavam Съжалявам
Big - Golyam Голям
Never – Nikoga Никога

Everything is about the money.
Vsichko opira do parite.
Всичко опира до парите.

I am never able to exchange this money at the bank.
Nikoga ne moga da obmenya tezi pari v bankata.
Никога не мога да обменя тези пари в банката.

I want to call my brother and my dad today
Iskam da se obadya na brat mi i bashta mi dnes
Искам да се обадя на брат ми и баща ми днес

I am sorry.
Sŭzhalyavam/izvinyavay
Съжалявам/извинявай

* *Prez* is an oft-used preposition in Bulgarian. It literally means "during."

*In Bulgarian, whenever pluralizing nouns, the ending changes to an *i*. For example, "book" / *kniga*, when pluralized, becomes *knigi*.

To return – Vrŭshtam Връщам
To live – Zhiveya Живея
New - Novo Ново
Child - Dete Дете
Up - Nagore Нагоре
Down - Nadolu Надолу
Of course - Razbira se Разбира се
Welcome - Dobre doshli Добре дошли
Without - Bez Без
There isn't – Nyama Няма
There aren't – Nyama takiva Няма такива
Excuse me - Izvinete Извинете
Also / too / as well - Sŭshto Също
Also / too / as well - Sŭstho taka Също така

It is impossible to live without problems.
Nevŭzmozhno e da se zhivee bez problemi.
Невъзможно е да се живее без проблеми.

I want to return to the United States.
Iskam da se vŭrna v Sŭedinenite shtati.
Искам да се върна в Съединените щати.

Excuse me, my child is here as well
Izvinete, deteto mi sŭshto e tuk
Извинете, детето ми също е тук

Of course I can come to the theater, and I want to sit together with you and with your sister
Razbira se, che moga da doĭda na teatŭr i iskam da sedna zaedno s teb i sŭs sestra ti
Разбира се, че мога да дойда на театър и искам да седна заедно с теб и със сестра ти

If you look under the table, you can see the new rug.
Ako poglednete pod masata, mozhete da vidite noviya kilim.
Ако погледнете под масата, можете да видите новия килим.

To allow - Pozvolyavam Позволявам
To believe - Vyarvam Вярвам
Morning - Sutrin Сутрин
Except - Osven Освен
To promise - Obeshtavam Обещавам
Good night - Leka nosht Лека нощ
To recognize - Razpoznavam Разпознавам
People - hora Хора
Far - Dalech далеч
To follow - Sledvam Следвам
Dog - Kuche Куче
Him - Nego Него
His - Negoviya неговия
Her - Tya Тя

I need to allow him to go with us.
Tryabva da mu pozvolya da trŭgne s nas.
Трябва да му позволя да тръгне с нас.

I can't recognize him.
Ne moga da go poznaya.
Не мога да го позная.

I believe everything except for this
Vyarvam na vsichko, osven na tova
Вярвам на всичко, освен на това

I need to put your cat to another chair
Tryabva da slozha kotkata vi na drug stol
Трябва да сложа котката ви на друг стол

I can see the sky from the window.
Vizhdam nebeto ot prozoretsa.
Виждам небето от прозореца.

The dog wants to follow me to the store.
Kucheto iska da me posledva do magazina.
Кучето иска да ме последва до магазина.

Man - Chovek Човек
To enter - Vlizam Влизам
To receive - Poluchavam Получавам
To prefer - Predpochitam Предпочитам
To put - Slagam Слагам
To move - Dvizha se Движа се
Less - Po-malko По-малко
Each / Every - Vseki Всеки
Left - Nalyavo Наляво
Right - Dyasno Дясно
Different – Razlichen Различен
Quickly - Bŭrzo Бързо
Country - Strana Страна

Come here quickly.
Ela tuk bŭrzo.
Ела тук бързо.

He is a different man now.
Toĭ veche e drug chovek.
Той вече е друг човек.

I see the sun in the morning from the kitchen
Sutrin Vizhdam slŭntseto ot kukhnyata
Сутрин Виждам Слънцето от кухнята

I want to pay less than you.
Iskam da plashtam po-malko ot teb.
Искам да плащам по-малко от теб.

I prefer to put this here.
Predpochitam da slozha tova tuk.
Предпочитам да сложа това тук.

Bulgaria is a beautiful country
Bǐlgariya ye krasiva strana
България е красива страна

To wish - Zhelaya Желая
To wish - Pozhelavam Пожелавам
Bad - Losho Лошо
To get - Poluchavam Получавам
To forget - Zabravyam Забравям
Person - Chovek Човек
Everybody / Everyone - Vsichki Всички
Everybody / Everyone - Vseki Всеки
Although - Vŭpreki che Въпреки че
Even though – Vŭpreki tova Въпреки това
To feel - Chuvstvam Чувствам
Great - Strakhotno Страхотно
To like - Haresvam Харесвам
Past – Minalo Минало
Through - Chrez Чрез
Throughout - Prez tsyaloto vreme През цялото време
Well - Dobre Добре

I don't want to wish anything bad
Ne iskam da pozhelavam nishto losho
Не искам да пожелавам нищо лошо

I must forget everybody from my past.
Tryabva da zabravya vsichki ot moeto minalo.
Трябва да забравя всички от моето минало.

To feel well I must take vitamins
Za da se chuvstvam dobre tryabva da priemam vitamini
За да се чувствам добре трябва да приемам витамини

I am close to the person behind you
Az sŭm blizo do choveka zad teb
Аз съм близо до човека зад теб

I go into the house from the front entrance and not through the yard.
Vlizam v kŭshtata ot glavniya vkhod, a ne prez dvora.
Влизам в къщата от главния вход, а не през двора.

Next – Sledva Следва
Next – Sledvasht Следващ
Behind - Otzad Отзад
Which - Koĭto Който
Restaurant - Restorant Ресторант
Bathroom - Banya Баня
Goodbye - Dovizhdane Довиждане
Bye – Chao Чао!
Small - Malŭk Малък
In front - Otpred Отпред

Goodbye, my friend.
Dovizhdane priyatelyu.
Довиждане приятелю.

Which is the best restaurant in the area?
Koĭ e naĭ-dobriyat restorant v raĭona?
Кой е най-добрият ресторант в района?

I can feel the heat.
Useshtam toplinata.
Усещам топлината.

I need to repair a part of the cabinet in the bathroom.
Tryabva da remontiram chast ot shkafa v banyata.
Трябва да ремонтирам част от шкафа в банята.

I want a car before the next year
Iskam kola do drugata godina
Искам кола до другата година

I like the house, but it is very small.
Kŭshtata mi kharesva, no e mnogo malka.
Къщата ми харесва, но е много малка.

There is a great person in front of me
Pred men stoi strakhoten chovek
Пред мен стои страхотен човек

To remove - Premahvam Премахвам
Beautiful - Krasivo Красиво
To lift - Vdigam Вдигам
Include / Including – Vklyuchvam Включвам
Belong - Prinadlezha Принадлежа
To check – Proveryavam Проверявам
So - Taka che Така че
Please - Molya Моля

She wants to remove this door, please
Tya iska da makhne tazi vrata, molya
Тя иска да махне тази врата, моля

We need to check the size of the house
Tryabva da proverim razmera na kŭshtata
Трябва да проверим размера на къщата

I want to lift this.
Iskam da vdigna tova.
Искам да вдигна това.

Can you please put the wood in the fire?
Mozhete li da slozhite dŭrvata v ogŭnya?
Можете ли да сложите дървата в огъня?

This doesn't belong here, I need to check again
Tova ne e ot tuk, tryabva da proverya otnovo
Това не е от тук, трябва да проверя отново

*In Bulgarian, the verb "need" has two definitions: *tryabva* and *nuzhno*. Both signify doing something out of necessity such as "need to," "have to," "should." Both could be used interchangeably, however, *tryabva* has more of a colloquial use. On the other hand, *nuzhno* means "must;" something you are forced to do. You will notice in some instances, throughout the program, these two Bulgarian verbs being used interchangeably.

*With the knowledge you've gained so far, now try to create your own sentences!

Real - Istinski Истински
Weather – Vreme Време
Size - Razmer Размер
Doesn't - Ne Не
Price Tsena Цена
To hold - Dŭrzha Държа
High – Vysokyy Високий
Low - Nisko Ниско
Hospital - Bolnitsa Болница

Is that a real diamond?
Tova istinski diamant li e?
Това истински диамант ли е?

This week the weather was very beautiful
Tazi sedmitsa vremeto beshe mnogo krasivo
Тази седмица времето беше много красиво

I can pay this although the price is expensive
Moga da platya tova, vŭpreki che tsenata e visoka
Мога да платя това, въпреки че цената е висока

Can you please hold my hand?
Mozhe li da me dŭrzhish za rŭkata?
Може ли да ме държиш за ръката?

Where is the hospital?
Kŭde e bolnitsata?
Къде е болницата?

The sun is high in the sky.
Slŭntseto e visoko v nebeto.
Слънцето е високо в небето.

Including everything is this price correct?
vsichko vklyucheno ,pravilna li e tazi tsena?
всичко Включено правилна ли е тази цена?

Building Bridges

In Building Bridges, we take six conjugated verbs that have been selected after studies I have conducted for several months in order to determine which verbs are most commonly conjugated, and which are then automatically followed by an infinitive verb. For example, once you know how to say, "I need," "I want," "I can," and "I like," you will be able to connect words and say almost anything you want more correctly and understandably. The following three pages contain these six conjugated verbs in first, second, third, fourth, and fifth person, as well as some sample sentences.

I want - Iskam Искам
I need / I must / I have to - Tryabva Трябва
I can - Moga Мога
I like - haresvam Харесвам
I go - Otivam Отивам
I have - Imam Имам

I want to go to my apartment
Iskam da otida v apartamenta si
Искам да отида в апартамента си

I can go with you to the bus station
Moga da otida s teb do avtogarata
Мога да отида с теб до автогарата

I need to walk outside the museum.
Tryabva da izlyaza izvŭn muzeya.
Трябва да изляза извън музея.

I like to eat oranges.
Obicham da yam portokali.
Обичам да ям портокали.

I am going to teach a class
Shte vodya klas
Ще водя клас

I have to speak to my teacher
Tryabva da govorya s moya uchitel
Трябва да говоря с моя учител

Please master *every* single page up until here prior to attempting the following few pages!

You want - Iskash Искаш
Do you want? - Iskash li? Искаш ли?

He wants - Toĭ iska Той иска

Does he want? - Iska li? Иска ли?

She wants - Tya iska Тя иска

Does she want? - Iska li? Иска ли?

We want - Iskame Искаме

Do we want? - Iskame li? Искаме ли?

They want - Te iskat Те искат

Do they want? - Iskat li? Искат ли?

You (plural) want - Vie iskate Вие искате

Do you (plural) want? - Iskate li? Искате ли?

You need - Imate li nuzhda Имате нужда

Do you need? - Imate nuzhda? Имате ли нужда?

He needs - Toy Ima nuzhda Той Има нужда

Does he need? - Ima li nuzhda? Има ли нужда?

She needs - Tya ima nuzhda Тя има нужда

Does she need? - Ima li nuzhda? Има ли нужда?

We need - Imame nuzhda Имаме нужда

Do we need? - Imame li nuzhda? Имаме ли нужда?

They need - Imat nuzhda Имат нужда

Do they need? - Nuzhdayat li se? Иуждаят ли се?

You (plural) need - Vie imate nuzhda Вие имате нужда

Do you (plural) need? - Imate li nuzhda? Имате ли нужда?

You can - Mozchesh Можеш

Can you? - Mozshesh li? Можеш ли?

He can - Toĭ mozhe Той може

Can he? - Mozhe li? Може ли?

She can - Tya mozhe Тя може

Can she? - Mozhe li? Може ли?

We can - Mozhem Можем

Can we? - Mozhem li? Можем ли?

They can - Te mogat Те могат

Can they? - Mogat li? Могат ли?

You (plural) can - Vie mozhete Вие можете

Can (plural) you? - Mozhete li? Можете ли?

You like - Haresvash Харесваш

Do you like? - Haresvash li? Харесваш ли?

He likes - Toĭ haresva Той харесва

Does he like? - Haresva li? Харесва ли?

She like - Tya haresva Тя харесва

Does she like? - Haresva li? Харесва ли?

We like - Haresvame Харесваме

Do we like? - Haresvame li? Харесваме ли?

They like - Te haresvat Те харесват

Do they like? - Haresvat li? Харесват ли?

You (plural) like - Vie haresvate Вие харесвате

Do you (plural) like? - Haresvate li? Харесвате ли?

You go - Otivash Отиваш

Do you go? - Otivash li? Отиваш ли?

He goes - Toĭ otiva Той отива

Does he go? - Otiva li? Отива ли?

She goes - Tya otiva Тя отива

Does she go? - Otiva li? Отива ли?

We go - Otivame Отиваме

Do we go? - Otivame li? Отиваме ли?

They go - Te otivat Те отиват

Do they go? - Otivat li? Отиват ли?

You (plural) go - Vie otivate Вие отивате

Do you (plural) go? - Otivate li? Отивате ли?

You have - Imash Имаш

Do you have? - Imash li? Имаш ли?

He has - Toĭ ima Той има

Does he have? - Ima li? Има ли?

She has - Tya ima Тя има

Does she have? - Ima li? Има ли?

We have - Imame Имаме

Do we have? - Imame li? Имаме ли?

They have - Imat Имат

Do they have? - Imat li? Имат ли?

You (plural) have - Vie imate Вие имате

Do you (plural) have? - Imate li? Имате ли?

Do you want to go?
Iskash li da trŭgvame?
Искаш ли да тръгваме

Does he want to fly?
Iska li da leti?
Иска ли да лети?

We want to swim.
Iskame da pluvame.
Искаме да плуваме

Do they want to run?
Iskat li da byagat?
Искат ли да бягат?

Do you need to clean?
Tryabva li da pochistish?
Трябва ли да почистиш?

She needs to sing a song.
Tya tryabva da izpee pesen.
Тя трябва да изпее песен

We need to travel.
Tryabva da pŭtuvame.
Трябва да пътуваме

They don't need to fight.
Te nyamat nuzhda da se biyat.
Те нямат нужда да се бият

You (plural) need to save your money.
Vie (Plural) tryabva da spestite parite si.
Вие трябва да спестите парите си.

Can you hear me?
Chuvash li me?
Чуваш ли ме?

He can dance very well.
Toĭ mozhe da tantsuva mnogo dobre.
Той може да танцува много добре

We can go out tonight.
Mozhem da izlezem tazi vecher.
Можем да излезем тази вечер

The fireman can break the door during an emergency.
Pozharnikaryat mozhe da razbie vratata po vreme na avariya.
Пожарникарят може да разбие вратата по време на авария.

Do you like to eat here?
Iskash li da hapnesh tuk?
Искаш ли да хапнеш тук?

He likes to spend time here.
Toĭ obicha da prekarva vremeto si tuk.
Той обича да прекарва времето си тук

We like to fix the house.
Obichame da opravyame kŭshtata.
Обичаме да оправяме къщата

They like to cook.
Obichat da gotvyat.
Обичат да готвят

You (plural) like to play soccer.
Vie (Plural) obichate da igraete futbol.
Вие обичате да играете футбол.

Do you go to the movies on weekends?
Khodite li na kino prez uikendite?
Ходите ли на кино през уикендите?

He goes fishing.
Toĭ otiva na ribolov.
Той отива на риболов

We are going to relax.
Otivame da se otpusnem.
Отиваме да се отпуснем

They go out to eat at a restaurant every day.
Vseki den izlizat da se khranyat v restorant.
Всеки ден излизат да се хранят в ресторант.

Do you have money?
Imash li pari?
Имаш ли пари?

She must look outside.
Tya tryabva da pogledne navŭn.
Тя трябва да погледне навън

We have to sign our names.
Tryabva da se podpishem s imenata si.
Трябва да се подпишем с имената си

They have to send the letter.
Te tryabva da izpratyat pismoto.
Те трябва да изпратят писмото

You (plural) have to stand in line.
Vie (Plural) tryabva da zastanete na opashka.
Вие трябва да застанете на опашка.

Other Useful Tools in the Bulgarian Language

Days of the Week Dni ot sedmitsata Дни от седмицата

Sunday - Nedelya Неделя
Monday - ponedelnik понеделник
Tuesday - vtornik вторник
Wednesday - Sryada Сряда
Thursday - Chetvŭrtŭk Четвъртък
Friday - Petŭk Петък
Saturday - Sŭbota Събота

Seasons Sezoni Сезони

Spring - Prolet Пролет
Summer - Lyato Лято
Autumn - Esen Есен
Winter - Zima Зима

Colors Tsvetove Цветове

Black - Cherno Черно
White - Byalo Бяло
Gray - Sivo Сиво
Red - Cherveno Червено
Blue - Sin'o Синьо
Yellow - Zhŭlto Жълто
Green - Zeleno Зелено
Orange - oranzhevo оранжево
Purple – Lilavo Лилаво
Brown - Kafyav Кафяв
Pink - Rozovo Розово
Light blue – Svetlo sinyo Светло синьо
Beige – Bezhovo Бежово
Dark grey - Tŭmno sivo Тъмно сиво
Dark - Tŭmno Тъмно
Light – Svetlo Светло

Numbers Chisla Числа

One - Edno Едно
Two - Dve Две
Three - Tri Три
Four - Chetiri Четири
Five - Pet Пет
Six - Shest Шест
Seven - Sedem Седем
Eight - Osem Осем
Nine - Devet Девет
Ten - Deset Десет

Cardinal Directions Kardinalni posoki Кардинални посоки

North - Sever Север
South - Yug Юг
East - Iztok Изток
West - Zapad Запад

Directions Posoki Посоки

Left – Lyavo - Ляво
Right – Dyasno – Дясно
Up – Nagore - Нагоре
Down – Nadolu - Надолу
Forward - Napred - Напред
Backwards – Nazad - Назад

Conversational Polish Quick and Easy
The Most Innovative Technique to Learn the Polish Language

YATIR NITZANY

The Polish Language

The official language of Poland is Polish. About 97 percent of Poland's citizens declare Polish as their native tongue, which is a very high amount of Poles that speak the language. At one point, Polish was more widespread than it is now, as Russian has overtaken the language in popularity in surrounding areas like Lithuania and Ukraine. However, Polish wasn't totally wiped out. That is, many people still know the language but don't speak it as frequently. German has greatly influenced the vocabulary of Polish, as Germany borders Poland. However, Germany isn't the only influential language. Belarus, Russia, the Czech Republic, and Slovakia all have had their fair share of influence on Polish as well.

Reading and Pronunciation

- *A* is pronounced as the English "u" in cult.
- *Ą* is pronounced as "on" or "om" but nasalized.
- *C* is pronounced as the English "ts" in cats.
- *Ć* is pronounced similar to the English "ch."
- *CZ* is pronounced as the English "ch" in church.
- *Ch* or *kh* (read paragraph below)
- *D* is pronounced as in English, but put your tongue against the front teeth and not against the teeth ridge.
- *DZ* is pronounced as the English "ds" in beds.
- *DŻ* is pronounced as the English "j" in jam.
- *DŹ* is pronounced as the English "j" in jeep.
- *E* is pronounced as the English "e" in ten.
- *Ę* is pronounced like "en" or "em" but nasalized.
- *G* is pronounced as the English "g" in girl.
- *H* is pronounced as *kh* (please read paragraph below).
- *I* is pronounced as the English "i" in fit.
- *J* is pronounced as the English 'y' in yet
- *Ł* is pronounced as the English 'w' in win
- *N* is pronounced as in English, but put your tongue against the front teeth and not against the teeth ridge.
- *Ń* is pronounced as in English "ny" in canyon.
- *O* is pronounced as the English "o" in cot.
- *R* is pronounced as the Scottish or German "r": trilled by vibration of the tongue.
- *RZ* is pronounced as the English "s" in pleasure.
- *SZ* is pronounced as the English "sh" in shoes.
- *Ś* is pronounced as the "sh" in English
- *T* is pronounced as in English, but put your tongue against the front teeth and not against the teeth ridge.
- *U* is pronounced as the English "oo" in boot.
- *Ó* is pronounced as the English "oo" in boot.
- *W* is pronounced the English "v" in van.
- *Ż* is pronounced as the English "s" in pleasure.
- *Ź* is pronounced as the "si" in vision.

The Program

I / I am - Ja / Ja jestem
With you - Z tobą / z wami
With him / with her - Z nim / Z nią
For you - Dla ciebie / (Plural) dla was
Without him - Bez niego
Without them - Bez nich
Always - Zawsze
I Was – (Ja) byłem
With us - Z nami
This - To
Is - Jest
Sometimes - Czasami
Today - Dzisiaj
Are you / you are - Jesteś / ty jesteś
Better - Lepiej
You - Ty (**singular**) / wy (**plural**)
His / hers - Jego/ Jej
He, he is – On
She, she is - Ona
From – Od/ z / ze

Sentences from the vocabulary (now you can speak the sentences and connect the words)

I am with you
Ja jestem z Tobą/ Ja jestem z Wami
I am always with her
Ja jestem zawsze z nią
I am from Poland
Ja jestem z Polski
Are you from Poland?
Jesteś z Polski?/ Jesteście z Polski?
This is for you
To jest dla Ciebie/ To jest dla Was
Are you at the house?
Jesteś w domu?
Sometimes I go without him.
Czasami idę bez niego.
Are you alone today?
Czy jesteś dziś sam?

I was - Ja byłem/byłam
To be - Być
The – (see footnote)
Same - Taki sam
Good - Dobrze/ dobre
Here - Tutaj
It's / is it? - To jest/ jest?
And - I
Between - Między
Now - Teraz
Later / After - Później/ Po
If - Jeśli
Yes - Tak
Tomorrow - Jutro
OK - Okej
Day - Dzień

I was home at 5pm
W domu byłem o 17:00
Between now and tomorrow.
Między teraz a jutrem.
It's better to be home later.
Lepiej być w domu później.
If this is good, then I am happy.
Jeśli to jest dobre, to jestem szczęśliwy.
Yes, you are very good
Tak, ty jesteś bardzo dobry
I was here with them
Ja byłem tutaj z nimi
You and I.
Ty i ja.
The same day
Taki/Ten sam dzień

*In the Polish language, there are no articles such as "the" nor "a." For example,
"at the house" / *w* (at) *domu* (home).

*The ending depends on the context.

*In Polish, "are you / you are" is *jesteś* / *ty jesteś*. However, the plural form is *jesteście* / *wy jesteście*.

Maybe - Może
I go - Ja pójdę
Even if - Nawet jeśli
Afterwards - Potem
Worse - Gorzej
Where - Gdzie/ Skąd
Everything - Wszystko
Somewhere - Gdzieś
What - Co/ Jaki/ Który
Almost - Prawie
There - Tam
Also / too / as well - Także

Afterwards is worse
Potem jest gorzej

Even if I go now
Nawet jeśli ja pójdę teraz

Where is everything?
Gdzie jest wszystko?

Maybe somewhere
Może gdzieś

What? I am almost there
Co? Ja jestem prawie tam

Where are you?
Gdzie jesteś?/ Gdzie jesteście?

This is for us.
To jest dla nas.

*This *isn't* a phrase book! The purpose of this book is *solely* to provide you with the tools to create *your own* sentences!

House / home - Dom
In / at - W/ na
Car - Samochód
Already - Już
Good morning - Dzień dobry
How are you? - Jak się masz?
Where are you from? - Skąd jesteś?/ Skąd jesteście?
Me - Mnie / ja
Hello - Cześć
What is your name? - Jakie jest Twoje imię?
How old are you? - Jak stary jesteś?
Son - Syn
Daughter - Córka
Your - Twoje
Very - Bardzo
Hard - Ciężko
Still - Wciąż
Then / so - Więc

She is not in the car, so maybe she is still at the house?
Nie ma jej w samochodzie, więc może jest jeszcze w domu?
I am already in the car with your son and daughter
Ja jestem już w samochodzie z Twoim synem i córką
Good morning, how are you today?
Dzień dobry, jak się dziś czujesz?
Hello, what is your name?
Cześć, Jakie jest Twoje imię?
How old are you?
Ile masz lat?
This is very hard, but it's not impossible
To jest bardzo ciężkie, ale to nie jest niemożliwe
Where are you from?
Skąd jesteś? / Skąd jesteście?

*"Your" / *twoje* is the nominative case, while *twoim* is used to indicate the instrumental case.

Się is used as a reflexive verb, pertaining to something that somebody has to do for oneself, herself/himself, themselves, ourselves, or itself. For example, *Czy może się Pan przesunąć?* literally means "Can you move?" but can be translated as, "Can you get yourself and move?"

Thank you - Dziękuje
For – Dla/ za /przez
A - (no equivalent)
This is - To jest
Time - Czas
But / however – Ale/ jednak
No / not - Nie
I am not - Ja jestem nie
Away- Z dala/ nieobecny
That - Że
Similar - Podobny
Other / another - Inny
Side - Strona
Until - Do
Yesterday - Wczoraj
Without us - Bez nas
Since - Od
Evening - Wieczór
Before - Przed

Thank you, Peter.
Dziękuję, Peter.

It's almost time
To jest prawie czas

I am not here, I am far away
Nie ma mnie tutaj, jestem daleko

That house is similar to ours.
Ten dom jest podobny do naszego.

I am from the other side
Ja jestem z innej strony

But I was here until late evening
Ale ja byłem tutaj do późnego wieczoru

Since the other day
Od innego dnia

I say / I am saying - Ja mówię
What time is it? - Jaki czas jest?
I want - Ja chcę
Without you - Bez ciebie/ Bez was
Everywhere /wherever – Wszędzie/ gdziekolwiek
I go / I am going - Ja idę/ zamierzać
With - Z
My - Mój
Cousin - (M) Kuzyn, (F) Kuzynka
I need / I must - Ja potrzebuję/Ja muszę
Right now – Właśnie teraz
Night - Noc
To see - Zobaczyć /widzieć
Light - Światło
Outside - Na zewnątrz
That is/ Is that - To jest/ czy jest
During - Podczas
I see / I am seeing - Ja widzę

I am saying no / I say no
Ja mówię nie
I want to see this during the day
Ja chcę zobaczyć to podczas dnia
I see this everywhere
Ja widzę to wszędzie
I am happy without any of my cousins here
Jestem szczęśliwy bez żadnego z moich kuzynów tutaj
I need to be there at night
Ja muszę być tam w nocy
You need to be at home.
Musisz być w domu.
I see light outside
Ja widzę światło na zewnątrz
What time is it right now?
Jaki czas jest właśnie teraz?

*Ja potrzebuję is used to signify "I need," while *ja muszę* signifies "I must." However, in this program both will be used interchangeably.

There are two forms used to express the case of "to see," and these are *zobaczyć* and *widzieć*. **Zobaczyć represents the perfective action / **Widzieć** represents the imperfective action. But again, this isn't a grammar book!

Place - Miejsce
Easy - Łatwy
To find - Znaleźć
To look for/to search - Szukać
Near / close - Obok, w pobliżu / blisko
To wait - Poczekać
To sell - Sprzedać
To use - Użyć
To know - Wiedzieć / znać
To decide - Postanowić
Between - Pomiędzy
Two - Dwa
To - Do, na, dla, aby żeby(or nothing)

This place is easy to find
To miejsce jest łatwe do znalezienia

I am saying to wait until tomorrow
Ja mówię aby poczekać do jutra

It's easy to sell this table
To jest łatwe, żeby sprzedać ten stół

I want to use this
Ja chcę, żęby użyć to

Where is the book?
Gdzie jest książka?

I need to look for you at the mall.
Muszę cię poszukać w centrum handlowym.

I must decide myself between both places
Ja muszę zdecydować się pomiędzy dwoma miejscami

I need to know that everything is OK
Ja potrzebuję wiedzieć, że wszystko jest okej

Is this place near?
Czy to miejsce jest blisko?

*The preposition "to" has several definitions in Polish.

Because - Ponieważ
To buy - Kupić
Both - Obie
Them / they / Their - Im/ oni / ich
Each / Every - Każdy
Book - Książka
Mine - Moja
To understand - Zrozumieć
Problem / Problems - Problem/ Problemy
I do / I am doing - Ja robię
Of - Z, na, o, ze
To look - Patrzeć
Myself – Sam, siebie, się
Enough - Wystarczająco
Food - Jedzenie
Water - Woda
Hotel - Hotel

I like this hotel because it's near the beach
Lubię ten hotel, ponieważ jest blisko plaży
I want to look at the view.
Chcę spojrzeć na widok.
I want to buy a bottle of water
Ja chcę kupić butelkę wody
Do it like this!
Zrób to tak!
That book is mine.
Ta książka jest moja.
I need to understand the problem
Ja muszę zrozumieć ten problem
From the hotel I have a view of the city
Z hotelu ja mam widok na miasto
I can work today
Ja mogę pracować dzisiaj
I do what I want.
Robię co chcę.

*To indicate "at the" or "of the," we use *na*.

*The endings of certain words vary depending on different cases. However, since this isn't a grammar book, this book won't teach you these skills.

I like - Ja lubię
There is / There are - Tam jest/ tam są
Family / Parents - Rodzina/ rodzice
Why - Dlaczego
To say - Powiedzieć
Something - Coś
To go - Chodzić /iść
Ready - Gotowy
Soon - Wkrótce
To work - Pracować
Who - Kto
Important - Ważne

I like to be at home with my parents
Ja lubię być w domu z moimi rodzicami
Why do I need to say something important?
Dlaczego muszę powiedzieć coś ważnego?
I am there with him
Ja jestem tam z nim
I am busy, but I need to be ready soon
Ja jestem zajęty, ale powinienem być gotowy wkrótce
I like to work
Ja lubię pracować
Who is there?
Kto jest tam?
I want to know if they are here.
Chcę wiedzieć, czy tu są.
I can go outside.
Mogę wyjść na zewnątrz.
There are seven dolls
Tam jest siedem lalek

*Powinienem is used to indicate "should."

*There are two forms used to indicate the verb "to go": *chodzić* and *iść*.

- *Chodzić* is used to indicate "going" but as in pattern habits. For example, when saying "I go to school every week," you would use *chodzić*.
- *Iść* is used to express "going" to a specific location. For example, when saying "I am going to the debate," you would use *iść*.

How much – Jak dużo
To take – Wziąć/skorzystać
With me - Ze mną
Instead - Zamiast
Only - Tylko
When - Kiedy
I can / Can I? - Ja mogę/ Mogę (ja)?
Or - Lub
Were - Były/ Byli
Without me - Beze mnie
Fast - Szybko
Slow - Wolno
Cold - Zimno
Inside - Wewnątrz
To eat - Jeść
Hot - Gorąco
To Drive - Jechać

How much money do I need to bring with me?
Ile pieniędzy muszę wziąć ze sobą?

I like bread instead of rice.
Lubię chleb zamiast ryżu.

Only when you can
Tylko kiedy Tymożesz

Go there without me.
Idź tam beze mnie.

I need to drive the car very fast or very slowly
Ja muszę jechać samochodem bardzo szybko lub bardzo wolno

It is cold in the library
Jest zimno w bibliotece

I like to eat a hot meal for my lunch.
Lubię zjeść ciepły posiłek na lunch.

*In regards to the conjugation of "can" for second, third, fourth person, etc., please see page 35.

To answer - Odpowiedzieć
To fly - Lecieć
Today - Dziś
To travel - Podróżwać
To learn – Nauczyć się
How - Jak
To swim - Pływać
To practice - Ćwiczyć
To play - Grać
To leave - Zostawić/opuścić
Many/much/a lot – Wiele/dużo
I go to - Ja idę do
First - Pierwszy
Time / Times - Czas/ Czasy

I need to answer many questions
Ja muszę odpowiedzieć na wiele pytań
I want to fly today
Ja chcę lecieć dziś
I need to learn to swim
Ja muszę nauczyć się pływać
I want to know everything about how to play better tennis
Ja chcę wiedzieć wszystko o tym jak grać lepiej tenis
Everything is about the money.
Wszystko kręci się wokół pieniędzy.
I want to leave my dog at home.
Chcę zostawić psa w domu.
I want to travel the world.
Chcę podróżować po świecie.
Since the first time
Od pierwszego razu
The children are yours
Dzieci są Twoje

*As regards the verb "to leave," *opuścić* is used to express "departing," "leaving a place," or "exiting," while *zostawić* is used to express the action of "leaving something behind."

*With the knowledge you've gained so far, now try to create your own sentences!

Nobody / anyone – Nikt/ ktokolwiek
Against - Przeciwko
Us - Nas
To visit - Odwiedzić
Mom / Mother - Mama
To give - Dać
Which - Które
To meet - Spotkać
Someone - Ktoś
Just - Tylko
To walk - Chodzić
Around – Wkoło/ dookoła
Towards – W kierunku/ku
Than - Niż
Nothing / Anything - Nic

Something is better than nothing
Coś jest lepsze niż nic
I am against him
Ja jestem przeciwko niemu
We go each week to visit my family
My jedziemy każdego tygodnia aby odwiedzić moją rodzinę
I need to give you something
Ja muszę dać Ci coś
Do you want to meet someone?
Czy ty chcesz spotkać kogoś?
I am here also on Wednesdays
Ja jestem tutaj również w środy
You do this every day?
Ty robisz to codziennie?
You need to walk around the school.
Musisz przejść się po szkole.

*When asking a question, *czy* is usually placed at the beginning of the sentence to indicate the case of "do" "do we?", "do you?", "does he?" etc. However, native Polish speakers usually don't use the *czy* case (please see page 35).

Ci is the "indirect object pronoun" of the pronoun, i.e. the person who is actually affected by the action that is being carried out.

I have – Ja mam
Don't - Nie
Friend - Przyjaciel
To borrow - Pożyczyć
To look like - Wyglądać jak
Grandfather - Dziadek
To want - Chcieć
To stay - Zostać
To continue - Kontynuować
Way - Droga
That's why – To jest dlatego
To show - Pokazać
To prepare - Przygotować
I am not going – Ja nie będę

Do you want to look like Arnold?
Czy Ty chcesz wyglądać jak Arnold?

I want to borrow this book for my grandfather
Ja chcę pożyczyć tę książkę dla mojego dziadka

I want to drive and to continue on this way to my house
Ja chcę jechać i kontynuować tą drogą do mojego domu

I want to stay in Krakow because I have a friend there.
Chcę zostać w Krakowie, bo mam tam przyjaciela.

I don't want to see anyone here
Nie chcę nikogo widzieć tutaj

I need to show you how to prepare breakfast
Ja muszę pokazać ci jak przygotować śniadanie

Why don't you have the book?
Dlaczego nie ty, masz książkę?

That is incorrect, I don't need the car today
To jest błędne, ja nie potrzebuje samochodu dzisiaj

*In Polish "I have" is *mam*, "you have" is *masz*. To learn more about these conjugations please see page 35.

*Ci is the "indirect object pronoun" of the pronoun, i.e. the person who is actually affected by the action that is being carried out.

To remember - Pamiętać
Polish - Polskie
Number - Numer
Hour - Godzina
Dark / darkness - Ciemny /ciemność
About - O
Grandmother - Babcia
Five - Pięć
Minute / minutes - Minuta/ minuty
More - Więcej
To think - Myśleć
To do - Robić
To come - Przyjść
To hear - Posłuchać
To hear - Usłyszeć
Last - Ostatni

I need to remember your number
Ja muszę zapamiętać twój numer

This is the last hour of darkness
To jest ostatnia godzina ciemności

I want to come with you.
Chcę iść z Tobą.

I can hear my grandmother speaking Polish.
Słyszę, jak moja babcia mówi po polsku.

I need to think about this more.
Muszę o tym więcej pomyśleć.

From here to there, it's only five minutes
Stąd do tamtąd, to jest tylko pięć minu

Where is the airport
Gdzie jest lotnisko

I want to sleep
Ja chcę spaćt

To leave - Odejść
Again – Ponownie
Poland - Polska
To bring - Przynieść
To try - Spróbować
To rent - Wynajmować
Without her - Bez niej
We are – My jesteśmy
To turn off - Wyłączyć
To ask - Prosić/zapytać
To stop – Zatrzymać
Permission - Pozwolenie
Early - Wcześnie
Long - Długie
Our - Nasz
On - Na

He must go and rent a house at the beach.
Musi iść i wynająć dom na plaży. We are here for a long time

We are here for a long time
My jesteśmy tutaj przez długi czas

I need to turn off the lights early tonight
Ja muszę wyłączyć światła wcześnie wieczorem

We want to stop here
My chcemy zatrzymać się tutaj

We are from Warsaw
My jesteśmy z Warszawy

Your doctor is in the same building.
Twój lekarz jest w tym samym budynku.

In order to leave you have to ask permission.
Aby wyjść, musisz poprosić o pozwolenie.

Our house is on the mountain.
Nasz dom jest na górze.

*To signify "again," we use ponownie. However, we can use *jeszcze raz* to signify "again," as well.

To open - Otworzyć
To buy - Kupić
To pay - Zapłacić
Last - Ostatni
Without - Bez
Sister - Siostra
To hope - Mieć nadzieję
To live - Żyć
Nice to meet you - Miło spotkać Ciebie
Name - Imię
Last name - Nazwisko
To return - Wrócić/powrócić
Enough - Dosyć
Door - Drzwi
To get to know - Poznać
Sad - Smutne

I need to open the door for my sister
Ja muszę otworzyć drzwi dla mojej siostry
I need to buy something
Ja muszę kupić coś
I want to meet your brothers.
Chcę poznać twoich braci.
Nice to meet you, what is your name and your last name?
Miło poznać Ciebie, jakie jest twoje imię i nazwisko?
We can hope for a better future.
Możemy mieć nadzieję na lepszą przyszłość.
It is impossible to live without problems.
Nie da się żyć bez problemów.
I want to return to the United States.
Chcę wrócić do Stanów Zjednoczonych.
Why are you sad right now?
Dlaczego jesteś smutna/y teraz?

**Wrócić* literally means "to come back."

*"To return (something/someone)" is *oddać*.

*This *isn't* a phrase book! The purpose of this book is *solely* to provide you with the tools to create *your own* sentences!

To happen – Zdarzyć/stać się
To order - Zamówić
To drink - Pić
Excuse me - Wybacz mi
Child - Dziecko
To begin / to start - Zacząć
To finish - Zakończyć
To help - Pomóc
To smoke - Palić
To love - Kochać
To talk / to speak - Rozmawiać/mówić

This must happen today
To musi się zdarzyć dziś

Excuse me, my child is here as well
Wybacz mi, moje dziecko jest tutaj również

I want to order a soup.
Chcę zamówić zupę.

We want to start the class soon.
Chcemy wkrótce rozpocząć zajęcia.

In order to finish at three o'clock this afternoon, I need to finish soon
Aby skończyć o trzeciej po południu, muszę skończyć wcześniej.

I want to learn how to speak perfect Polish.
Chcę nauczyć się mówić perfekcyjnie po polsku.

I don't want to smoke again
Ja nie chcę palić ponownie

I need you
Ja potrzebuję cię

I love you
Ja kocham cię

I see you
Ja widzę cię

I want to help
Ja chcę pomóc

To read - Czytać/przeczytać
To write - Pisać
To teach - Uczyć
To close - Zamknąć
To turn on - Włączyć
To prefer - Woleć
To put - Położyć
Less - Mniej
Sun - Słońce
Month - Miesiąc
I talk – Rozmawiać/ Mówić
Exact – Dokładnie/wiernie
To choose - Wybrać
To allow - Pozwolić/umożliwić
Man – Człowiek, mężczyzna / **Woman** - Kobieta

I need this book to learn how to read and write in Polish.
Potrzebuję tej książki, aby nauczyć się czytać i pisać po polsku.
I want to teach English in Poland.
Chcę uczyć angielskiego w Polsce.
I want turn on the lights and close the door.
Chcę zapalić światło i zamknąć drzwi.
I want to pay less than you.
Chcę płacić mniej niż ty.
I prefer to put this here.
Wolę umieścić to tutaj.
I speak with the boy and the girl in Russian
Ja rozmawiam z chłopcem i dziewczyną po rosyjsku
There is sun outside today.
Na ulicy dzisiaj jest słońce.
Is it possible to know the exact date?
Czy to możliwe, aby znać dokładną datę?
I need to allow him to go with us.
Muszę pozwolić mu iść z nami.
He is a different man now.
Jest teraz innym człowiekiem.

**Pozwolić* means "to allow," while *umożliwić* means "to permit."

*"Man" is *człowiekiem*; however *mężczyzna* can be used to signify a "man," as well.

To exchange - Wymiana
To call - Zadzwonić
Brother - Brat
Dad - Tata
To sit - Siedzieć
Together - Razem
To change - Zmienić
Of course - Oczywiście
Welcome - Witam
During - Podczas
Years - Lata
Sky - Niebo
Up - W górę
Down - W dół
Sorry - Przepraszam
To follow – Podążać/ Iść za
Her - Nią/ Jej
Big - Duże
New - Nowe
Never - Nigdy

I am never able to exchange this money at the bank.
Nigdy nie jestem w stanie wymienić tych pieniędzy w banku.
I want to call my brother and my dad today
Ja chcę zadzwonić do mojego brata i mojego taty dzisiaj
Of course I can come to the theater, and I want to sit together with you and with your sister
Oczywiście ja mogę przyjść do teatru, i ja chcę siedzieć razem z tobą i twoją siostrą
If you look under the table, you can see the new rug.
Jeśli zajrzysz pod stół, zobaczysz nowy dywan.
I am sorry.
Przepraszam
I can see the sky from the window
Ja mogę widzieć niebo z okna
The dog wants to follow me to the store.
Pies chce iść za mną do sklepu.

*The definition of *zejść* is "to go down." However, *zejść na dół* means "to descend." In English the term "to go down" isn't commonly used; however, in other languages that term is quite prevalent.

To believe - Wierzyć
Morning - Rano
Except - Wyjątek/poza
To promise - Obiecać
Good night - Dobranoc
To recognize – Rozpoznać/uznać
People - Ludzie
To move - Przenieść
Far - Daleko
Different - Różne, inne
Quickly - Szybko
To receive - Otrzymać
Throughout - Przez
Tonight - Dziś wieczorem
Through - Poprzez
Him / his - Go / jego
Doesn't - Nie

I believe everything except for this
Ja wierzę, we wszystko, z wyjątkiem tego
Come here quickly.
Chodź tu szybko.
I can't recognize him.
Nie mogę go rozpoznać.
I see the sun in the morning from the kitchen
Ja widzę słońce rano z kuchni
I want his car
Ja chcę ten samochód
The plant is on our table
Roślina jest na naszym stole
I go into the house from the front entrance and not through the yard.
Wchodzę do domu przednim wejściem, a nie przez podwórze.
I want a car before the next year
Ja chcę samochód przed następnym rokiem

*There are two forms used to express "next," *blisko* and *następny*. ***Blisko/niedaleko*** means "next to," "near," or "close." ***Następny*** is used to express "the next," or "the following."

Różne means "different," while *innym* means "another."

173

To wish - Życzyć
Bad - Zły
To get - Uzyskać
To forget - Zapomnieć
Everybody / everyone – Wszyscy/ każdy
To feel - Czuć
Great - Wspaniałe
Next - Następne/blisko
To like - Lubić
In front – Z przodu
Person - Osoba
Behind - Za
Well - Cóż
Restaurant - Restauracja
Bathroom - Łazienka
Part - Część
Goodbye - Żegnaj
Small - Mały

I don't want to wish anything bad
Ja nie chcę życzyć niczego złego
I must forget everybody from my past
Ja muszę zapomnieć wszystkich z mojej przeszłości
To feel well I must take vitamins
Aby dobrze się czuć, muszę brać witaminy
I am close to the person behind you
Ja jestem niedaleko osoby za tobą
There is a great person in front of me
Tu jest wspaniała osoba przede mną
Goodbye my friend.
Do widzenia mój przyjacielu.
Which is the best restaurant in the area?
Która restauracja jest najlepsza w okolicy?
I can feel the heat.
Czuję ciepło.
I need to repair a part of the cabinet of the bathroom.
Muszę naprawić część szafki w łazience.
I like the house, but it is very small.
Podoba mi się ten dom, ale jest bardzo mały.

Tobą is the dative form of "you."

To remove - Usunąć
Please - Proszę
Beautiful - Piękne
To lift - Podnieść
Include / including - Zawiera
Belong - Należeć
To hold - Trzymać
To check - Sprawdzić
Doesn't - Nie
Real - Prawdziwy
Week - Tydzień
Size - Rozmiar
Even though - Nawet jeśli
So - Tak (is used to express "so big," "so small," or "so fast."),
So - Więc (as in "then")
Price - Cena

She wants to remove this door, please
Ona chce usunąć te drzwi, proszę
This doesn't belong here, I need to check again
To nie należy tutaj, ja muszę to sprawdzić jeszcze raz
This week the weather was very beautiful
W tym tygodniu pogoda była bardzo piękna
Is that a real diamond?
Czy to prawdziwy diament?
We need to check the size of the house
Musimy sprawdzić rozmiar domu
I want to lift this.
Chcę to podnieść.
The sun is high in the sky.
Słońce jest wysoko na niebie.
Can you please put the wood in the fire?
Czy możesz dołożyć drewno do ognia?
Can you please hold my hand?
Czy możesz proszę potrzymać mnie za rękę?
I can pay this although the price is expensive
Ja mogę zapłacić to chociaż cena jest droga

*Była is used to express "was."

*Jak duży jest dom literally means "how big is the house."

Building Bridges

In Building Bridges, we take six conjugated verbs that have been selected after studies I have conducted for several months in order to determine which verbs are most commonly conjugated, and which are then automatically followed by an infinitive verb. For example, once you know how to say, "I need," "I want," "I can," and "I like," you will be able to connect words and say almost anything you want more correctly and understandably. The following three pages contain these six conjugated verbs in first, second, third, fourth, and fifth person, as well as some sample sentences. Please master the entire program up until here prior to venturing onto this section.

I want - Chcę
I need - Potrzebuję
I can - Mogę
I like - Lubię
I go - Idę
I have - Mam
I must/I have to - Muszę

I want to go to my apartment
Ja chcę iść do mojego mieszkania

I can go with you to the bus station
Ja mogę iść z tobą na dworzec autobusowy

I need to leave the museum.
Muszę opuścić muzeum.

I like to eat oranges.
Lubię jeść pomarańcze.

I am going to teach a class
Ja zamierzam uczyć klasę

I have to speak to my teacher
Ja muszę porozmawiać z moim nauczycielem

Please master *every* single page up until here prior to attempting the following two pages!

You want - Ty chcesz/ Wy checie

Do you want? - Czy ty chcesz? / Czy wy chcecie?

He wants / does he want - On chce/ Czy on chce?

She wants / does she want - Ona chce /Czy ona chce?

We want / do we want - My chcemy /Czy my chcemy?

They want / do they want - Oni chcą /Czy oni chcą?

You (plural) want? - Wy chcecie/ Czy wy chcecie?

You need - Ty potrzebujesz/ Wy potrzebujecie

Do you need? - Czy ty potrzebujesz? / Czy wy potrzebujecie?

He needs / does he need - On potrzebuje / Czy on potrzebuje?

She needs / does she need - Ona potrzebuje /Czy ona potrzebuje?

We need / do we need - My potrzebujemy / Czy my potrzebujemy?

They need / do they need - Oni potrzebują /Czy oni potrzebują?

You (plural) need - Wy potrzebujecie/ Czy wy potrzebujecie?

You can - Ty mozesz/ Wy możecie

Can you? - Czy ty możesz? / Czy wy możecie?

He can / can he - On może / Czy on może?

She can / can she - Ona może / Czy ona może?

We can / can we - My możemy / czy my możemy?

They can / can they - Oni mogą / Czy oni mogą?

You (plural) want - Wy checie/ czy wy chcecie?

You like - Ty Lubisz/ Wy idziecie

Do you like? - Czy Ty Lubisz? / Czy wy lubicie?

He likes / does he like - On lubi /Czy on lubi?

She likes / does she like - Ona lubi / Czy ona lubi?

We like / do we like - My lubimy /Czy my lubimy?

They like / do they like - Oni lubią /Czy oni lubią?

You (plural) like - Wy lubicie/ Czy wy lubicie?

You go – Ty Idziesz/ Wy Idziecie

Do you go? - Czy idziesz? / Czy idziecie?

He goes / does he go - On idzie /Czy on idzie?

She goes / does she go - Ona idzie /Czy ona idzie?

We go / do we go - My idziemy /Czy my idziemy?

They go / do they go - Oni idą /Czy oni idą?

You (plural) go - Wy idziecie/ Czy wy idziecie?

You have - Ty masz/ Wy macie

Do you have? - Czy ty masz? / Czy wy macie?

He has / does he have - On ma /Czy on ma?

She has / does she have - Ona ma/Czy ona ma?

We have / do we have - My mamy/Czy my mamy?

They have / do they have - Oni mają /Czy oni mają?

You (plural) have - Wy macie/ Czy wy macie?

You must - Ty musisz/ Wy musicie

Must you? - Czy ty musisz?/ Czy wy musicie?

He must/ must he? - On musi / Czy on musi?

She must/ must she? - Ona musi/Czy Ona musi?

We must/ must we? - My musimy/Czy my musimy?

They must/ must they? - Oni muszą / Czy oni muszą?

You (plural) must? - Wy muście / Czy wy muście?

Do you want to go?
Czy ty chcesz iść?

Does he want to fly?
Czy on chce lecieć?

We want to swim
My chcemy pływać

Do they want to run?
Czy oni chcą biegać?

Do you need to clean?
Czy ty potrzebujesz posprzątać?

She needs to sing a song
Ona potrzebuje zaśpiewać piosenkę

We need to travel
My potrzebujemy podróżować

They don't need to fight
Oni nie muszą walczyć

You (plural) need to save your money.
Wy musicie oszczędzać pieniądze.

Can you hear me?
Czy ty słyszysz mnie?

He can dance very well
On potrafi tańczyć bardzo dobrze

We can go out tonight
Możemy wyjść dziś wieczorem

The fireman can break the door during an emergency.
Strażak może wyłamać drzwi w sytuacji awaryjnej.

Do you like to eat here?
Czy ty lubisz jeść tutaj?

He likes to spend time here
On lubi spędzać czas tutaj

We like to fix the house
My lubimy naprawiać ten dom

They like to cook
Oni lubią gotować

You (plural) like to play soccer.
Wy lubicie grać w piłkę nożną.

Do you go to the movies on weekends?
Czy chodzisz do kina w weekendy?

He goes fishing
On idzie łowić ryby

We are going to relax
My zamierzamy się zrelaksować

They go out to eat at a restaurant everyday.
Codziennie wychodzą coś zjeść do restauracji.

Do you have money?
Czy ty masz pieniądze?

He must go to sleep
On musi iść spać

She must look outside
Ona musi patrzeć na zewnątrz

We have to sign our names
My musimy podpisać nasze imiona

They have to send the letter
Oni muszą wysłać list

You (plural) have to stand in line.
Wy musicie stać w kolejce.

Other Useful Tools in the Polish Language

Days of the Week
Sunday - Niedziela
Monday - Poniedziałek
Tuesday - Wtorek
Wednesday - Środa
Thursday - Czwartek
Friday - Piątek
Saturday - Sobota

Months
January - Styczeń
February - Luty
March - Marzec
April - Kwiecień
May - Maj
June - Czerwiec
July - Lipiec
August - Sierpień
September - Wrzesień
October - Październik
November - Listopad
December - Grudzień

Seasons
Spring - Wiosna
Summer - Lato
Autumn - Jesień
Winter - Zima

Cardinal Directions
North - Północ
South - Południe
East - Wschód
West – Zachód

Colors
Black - Czarny
White - Biały
Gray - Szary
Red - Czerwony

Blue - Niebieski
Yellow - Żółty
Green - Zielony
Orange - Pomarańczowy
Purple - Fioletowy
Brown - Brązowy

Numbers
One - Jeden
Two - Dwa
Three - Trzy
Four - Cztery
Five - Pięć
Six - Sześć
Seven - Siedem
Eight - Osiem
Nine - Dziewięć
Ten - Dziesięć
Eleven - Jedenaście
Twelve - Dwanaście
Thirteen - Trzynaście
Fourteen - Czternaście
Fifteen - Piętnaście
Sixteen - Szesnaście
Seventeen - Siedemnaście
Eighteen - Osiemnaście
Nineteen - Dziewiętnaście
Twenty - Dwadzieścia
Thirty - Trzydzieści
Forty - Czterdzieści
Fifty - Pięćdziesiąt
Sixty - Sześćdziesiąt
Seventy - Siedemdziesiąt
Eighty - Osiemdziesiąt
Ninety - Dziewięćdziesiąt
One hundred - Sto
Thousand - Tysiąc
Million - Milion
Billion - Miliard

Conclusion

Congratulations! You have completed all the tools needed to master the Russian, Bulgarian, Ukrainian and the Polish language, and I hope that this has been a valuable learning experience. Now you have sufficient communication skills to be confident enough to embark on a visit to a Slavic speaking country, impress your friends, and boost your resume so *good luck*.

This program is available in other languages as well, and it is my fervent hope that my language learning programs will be used for good, enabling people from all corners of the globe and from all cultures and religions to be able to communicate harmoniously. After memorizing the required three hundred and fifty words, please perform a daily five-minute exercise by creating sentences in your head using these words. This simple exercise will help you grasp conversational communications even more effectively. Also, once you memorize the vocabulary on each page, follow it by using a notecard to cover the words you have just memorized and test yourself and follow *that* by going back and using this same notecard technique on the pages you studied during the previous days. This repetition technique will assist you in mastering these words in order to provide you with the tools to create your own sentences.

Every day, use this notecard technique on the words that you have just studied.

Everything in life has a catch. The catch here is just consistency. If you just open the book, and after the first few pages of studying the program, you put it down, then you will not gain anything. However, if you consistently dedicate a half hour daily to studying, as well as reviewing what you have learned from previous days, then you will quickly realize why this method is the most effective technique ever created to become conversational in a foreign language. My technique works! For anyone who doubts this technique, all I can say is that it has worked for me and hundreds of others.

Congratulations! Now You Are on Your Own!

If you merely absorb the required three hundred and fifty words in this book, you will then have acquired the basis to become conversational in Russian, Bulgarian, and Polish! After memorizing these three hundred and fifty words, this conversational foundational basis that you have just gained will trigger your ability to make improvements in conversational fluency at an amazing speed! However, in order to engage in quick and easy conversational communication, you need a special type of basics, and this book will provide you with just that.

Unlike the foreign language learning systems presently used in schools and universities, along with books and programs that are available on the market today, that focus on *everything* but being conversational, *this* method's sole focus is on becoming conversational in a foreign language. Once you have successfully mastered the required words in this book, there are two techniques that if combined with these essential words, can further enhance your skills and will result in you improving your proficiency tenfold. *However*, these two techniques will only succeed *if* you have completely and successfully absorbed the three hundred and fifty words. *After* you establish the basis for fluent communications by memorizing these words, you can enhance your conversational abilities even more if you use the following two techniques.

The first step is to attend a language class (in whichever one of these languages which you just mastered) that will enable you to sharpen your grammar. You will gain additional vocabulary and learn past and present tenses, and if you apply these skills that you learn in the class, together with the three hundred and fifty words that you have previously memorized, you will be improving your conversational skills tenfold. You will notice that, conversationally, you will succeed at a much higher rate than any of your classmates. A simple second technique is to choose foreign subtitles while watching a movie. If you have successfully mastered and grasped these three hundred and fifty words, then the combination of the two—those words along with the subtitles—will aid you considerably in putting all the grammar into perspective, and again, conversationally, you will improve tenfold.

Once you have established a basis of quick and easy conversation in these 3 languages with those words that you just attained, every additional word or grammar rule you pick up from there on will be gravy. And these additional words or grammar rules can be combined with the three hundred and fifty words, enriching your conversational abilities even more. Basically, after the research and studies I've conducted with my method over the years, I came to the conclusion that in order to become conversational, you first must learn the words and *then* learn the grammar.

The Russian, Bulgarian, and Polish languages are compatible with the mirror translation technique. Likewise, with *this* language, you can use this mirror translation technique in order to become conversational, enabling you to communicate even more effortlessly. Mirror translation is the method of translating a phrase or sentence, word for word from English to another foreign language, by using these imperative words that you have acquired through this program (such as the sentences I used in this book). Latin languages, Middle Eastern languages, and Slavic languages, along with a few others, are also compatible with the mirror translation technique. Though you won't be speaking Shakespearean, you will still be fully understood and, conversation-wise, be able to get by just fine.

NOTE FROM THE AUTHOR

Thank you for your interest in my work. I encourage you to share your overall experience of this book by posting a review. Your review can make a difference! Please feel free to describe how you benefited from my method or provide creative feedback on how I can improve this program. I am constantly seeking ways to enhance the quality of this product, based on personal testimonials and suggestions from individuals like you. In order to post a review, please check with the retailer of this book.

Thanks and best of luck,
Yatir Nitzany

www.ingramcontent.com/pod-product-compliance
Lightning Source LLC
Chambersburg PA
CBHW070141080526
44586CB00015B/1785